African Americans and the Gettysburg Campaign

Sesquicentennial Edition

James M. Paradis

THE SCARECROW PRESS, INC.
Lanham • Toronto • Plymouth, UK
2013

Published by Scarecrow Press, Inc.
A wholly owned subsidiary of The Rowman & Littlefield Publishing Group, Inc.
4501 Forbes Boulevard, Suite 200, Lanham, Maryland 20706
www.rowman.com

10 Thornbury Road, Plymouth PL6 7PP, United Kingdom

British Library Cataloguing in Publication Information Available

Library of Congress Cataloging-in-Publication Data
Paradis, James M., 1949–
  African Americans and the Gettysburg Campaign / James M. Paradis. —
Sesquicentennial ed.
     p. cm.
  Includes bibliographical references and index.
  ISBN 978-0-8108-8336-9 (pbk. : alk. paper) — ISBN 978-0-8108-8337-6
(ebook)
  1. Gettysburg Campaign, 1863—Participation, African American. 2. United States—
History—Civil War, 1861–1865—Participation, African American. 3.
African American soldiers—History—19th century. I. Title.
  E475.51.P18 2013
  973.7'415—dc23

                                                                    2012015746

∞™ The paper used in this publication meets the minimum requirements of
American National Standard for Information Sciences—Permanence of Paper
for Printed Library Materials, ANSI/NISO Z39.48-1992.

Printed in the United States of America

To my mentor, Dr. Russell F. Weigley,
who encouraged me to write it, and to the
long-forgotten African Americans
whose stories inspired it.

~

Contents

~

Figures and Photos

Figures

Photos

~

Foreword

What has been apparent for too long is the small number of African Americans visiting national parks that commemorate the Civil War or participating in seminars and tours highlighting sites, personalities, and events associated with a defining era in our national experience. At Gettysburg, this lack of interest by black America in the National Military Park, the borough, and Adams County has long been a concern. This should not be.

In 1860, both in the county and in the borough, there was a significant African American population. Located in a free state bordering a slave state, Adams County was an important stop on the "underground railroad." Thousands of blacks were present on the battlefield in supporting roles in both armies. And on November 19, 1863, President Abraham Lincoln in his Gettysburg Address redefined the Union war goals. In doing so, he reached back to the Declaration of Independence. With it, "all men are created equal" and possess the unalienable right to liberty. The significance of Gettysburg to all people, with emphasis on black America, is masterfully addressed by historian James M. Paradis in *African Americans and the Gettysburg Campaign*. The story of the borough and county's black community caught up in an epic struggle makes for narrative history at its best. The book is people and site oriented. As such, it encourages the ever-increasing number of park and area visitors that delight in heritage tourism to view sites associated with Gettysburg's African American community. To facilitate the visitors' desire to walk in the steps of history, the author has included a chapter highlighting black-associated sites and structures, along with two very useful tour maps.

Edwin C. Bearss
Chief Historian Emeritus
National Park Service

~

Acknowledgments

To the First Edition

Many wonderful people gave up their time and shared their expertise with me when I wrote the first edition of *African Americans and the Gettysburg Campaign*. Their influence continues to influence the sesquicentennial edition. Those I thanked then included Michael Musick and Jill Abraham at the National Archives; Dr. Richard Summers of the U.S. Army Military History Institute; and Gettysburg National Military Park staff John Heiser, Scott Hartwig, Troy Harman, Greg Goodell, Dean Knudsen, and Elizabeth Trescott.

The staff of the Adams County Historical Society, especially Tim Smith and Gerald R. Bennett, helped very much. Craig Caba, Debra Sandoe Mc-Causlin, Andy Waskie, and Jeanne O. Bohn, Jean Odom, and William A. Frassanito also shared, as did Gabor S. Borritt, Kent Masterson Brown, and Gary Kross.

Arleen Thompson created four original maps. Several people read the manuscript and gave helpful comments, including Edwin C. Bearss, William A. Gladstone, Betty Dorsey Myers, and Peter C. Vermilyea. Ed Bearss also volunteered to write a foreword.

I enjoyed the support of both of the schools at which I teach—Doane Academy and Arcadia University—particularly from Anita Washington, Patricia Mesthos, John Corra, and Richard Ercholani. Steve Paradis and Amy Nowack Paradis provided technical support.

To the Sesquicentennial Edition

I am thankful to Martin Gordon, Bennett Graff, Jayme Bartles Reed, Jin Yu, and Rayna Andrews of Scarecrow Press for their support throughout this project.

Thanks go to Greg Goodell and Paul Shevchuk for help with the photo archives at Gettysburg National Military Park and to John Heiser for help with the print archives there. Thanks also to Richard Saylor for helping to locate at the Pennsylvania Commonwealth archives letters between David Wills and Governor Andrew Curtain.

I enjoyed wonderful support from my Doane Academy family. John Mc-Gee, head of the school, allowed me the time and facilities to work on the manuscript. Jack Newman helped with photos and illustrations, and Pat Blair helped type. At Arcadia, I enjoyed the support of history department chair Geoff Haywood and the assistance of interlibrary loan coordinator Jay Slott. Anita Washington's priceless help with typing and with computer operations got me through this process. Thanks also to Amy Nowack Paradis for additional computer help.

Finally, thank you Lorraine, for doing all of the things you did to free me to write this.

~

Introduction to the First Edition

In June 1863, Confederate troops splashed across the Potomac and pushed on into Pennsylvania. A month later, they crossed back into Virginia. Between those two river crossings, more than fifty thousand Americans were killed, wounded, or missing in action. Thousands of civilians fled their homes in the campaign that climaxed in the greatest battle fought in the Western Hemisphere.

Gettysburg stands as an important chapter in African American history. Anyone who stood on the Gettysburg battlefield during the three-day engagement would have seen thousands of African Americans actively performing essential roles both as soldiers in the armies and as civilians caught in their paths.

In the years following the great battle, African Americans visited Gettysburg in large numbers. They understood the meaning of the Battle of Gettysburg and the Gettysburg Address in their history. Attitudes changed, however. As Southerners began to put behind them the stinging memory of defeat at Gettysburg, it became more and more a place for Southerners to celebrate the bravery and fortitude of their ancestors. The Confederate battle flag, a symbol increasingly viewed by blacks as unfriendly, began to wave more freely at the site.

In a nation that desired to move forward together, past conflict had to be forgotten. In the rush to reunion, the differences between the two sides and the divisive issues of slavery and emancipation had to be swept aside. The fascination with battle tactics and personalities and the increased emphasis on reconciliation between the North and the South came to overshadow consideration of the causes and meaning of the war. The "new birth of freedom" and "the proposition that all men are created equal" became almost-forgotten aspects of the battle and of the Civil War itself. Americans both black and white came to hold the mistaken beliefs that blacks did not fight in the Gettysburg Campaign and that no blacks were wounded or killed opposing the invasion. Black Americans began to feel a distance from the Civil War in general and Gettysburg in particular, and their flow of pilgrimages to this hallowed ground dried to a trickle. Those who made the journey often found the visit confusing and unfulfilling. They did not find it relevant or meaningful to them.

This book attempts to set the record straight, by filling in the missing pieces involving African Americans and the Gettysburg Campaign and by helping African Americans take back their own history in this dramatic struggle for freedom.

~

Introduction to Sesquicentennial Edition

All during the writing of *African Americans and the Gettysburg Campaign*, I found myself continually changing the manuscript because of new information that I wanted to include. Even as the manuscript traveled to the editor, new scholarship was bringing new information to light. Someone once said that an author never really finishes a book; he just reaches a point where he gives up. That was certainly true in this case.

The coming of the sesquicentennial of the Civil War provides an opportunity to revise and expand on the first edition. Many new works have been published, some exploring new areas previously neglected by historians. Others have lent greater insight into matters familiar to students of the Gettysburg Campaign or African American history.

Margaret Creighton, in *The Colors of Courage*, presented an exceptionally sensitive treatment of Gettysburg's African Americans caught in the maelstrom. Gabor Boritt gave new meaning to the Gettysburg Address in *The Gettysburg Gospel*. Kent Masterson Brown, in *Retreat from Gettysburg: Lee, Logistics and the Pennsylvania Campaign*, gave new insight into the role of African Americans accompanying the Confederate Army. Scott Mingus, in *Flames beyond Gettysburg*, shed new light on the campaign of General John B. Gordon and the Battle of Wrightsville. George Nagle did an exhaustive study of the role of African Americans in defending Harrisburg in *Year of Jubilee: Men of Muscle*. Debra Sandoe McCauslin, in *Reconstructing the Past*, uncovered more of the mystery of the Yellow Hill community. Dr. Robert G. Slawson brought to light the participation of African Americans in the medical service in his pioneering work *Prologue to Change: African Americans in Medicine in the Civil War Era*. Harriette Rinaldi, in *Born at the Battlefield of Gettysburg: An African American Family Saga*, told for the first time the story of a black woman who gave birth on that hallowed ground as the conflict raged.

This and other scholarship have enriched the understanding of the role of African Americans and the Gettysburg Campaign. Let us hope that the sesquicentennial spreads the word.

CHAPTER ONE

~

African Americans at Gettysburg before the War

Before the Storm

African Americans have been a part of Gettysburg since the nation was born. The first settler in this area, Samuel Gettys, owned slaves. He built a tavern here in 1762. In the spring of 1774, Alexander Dobbin, a white Presbyterian minister, purchased two hundred acres of land in Cumberland Township in what is now the southern part of the town of Gettysburg. He returned in 1776 to build a home that would double as a classical school. His two slaves did the work of constructing this fine stone building. These were possibly the first two black residents of what would be the borough of Gettysburg. They may also have begun erecting on the property a stone wall along a slight rise that would one day be named Cemetery Ridge. "Four score and seven years" later, another stretch of stone wall, also built by black hands, would affect the outcome of the Battle of Gettysburg, as it sheltered Union soldiers poised to repel "Pickett's Charge" at the climax of the Battle of Gettysburg.[1]

About 1786, James Gettys, Samuel's son, founded the borough that was to be named after him. His slave, Sydney O'Brien, would be one of the first black residents of the town. Some time after Gettys's death, she obtained her freedom. In 1833, she purchased a half-lot for her home. Her house, which no longer stands, was on South Washington Street on what is now the road surface of Breckinridge Street. Sydney O'Brien's descendents live in the Gettysburg area to this day.[2]

Pennsylvania, a "free state," had a gradual emancipation. The 1780 Act for the Gradual Abolition of Slavery provided for the emancipation of enslaved

1

people in Pennsylvania upon their reaching the age of twenty-eight. Children of slaves would not be free until their twenty-eighth birthday. By the 1820s, a number of slaves still lived in the state, but by the 1840s, slavery had practically disappeared there. Many black residents of Gettysburg were born in neighboring Maryland, a slave state. Some may have been escaped slaves, but many who had obtained their freedom chose to come to Gettysburg for economic, educational, or social advancement. One the most notable of these was Clem Johnson. Johnson had been a slave in Maryland, but in 1831, his owner filed a document at the Adams County Courthouse in Gettysburg, stating,

> Whereas I, Francis Scott Key of the District of Columbia, being the owner of a certain man of colour called Clem Johnson, now in Gettysburg in the State of Pennsylvania . . . emancipate the said Clem Johnson & having agreed with him to leave him in the state of Pennsylvania and free to continue there, or to go wherever he may please, now therefore in consideration of five dollars to me in hand paid & for other good causes & considerations I hereby do manumit and let free the said Clem Johnson aged about forty five years.[3]

This former owner was the same Francis Scott Key who, years before, had written the words to "The Star-Spangled Banner."

As slavery died out in Pennsylvania, a vibrant community of free African Americans developed in Gettysburg. Members of this community spoke out against slavery and aided fugitive slaves in their flight to freedom via the Underground Railroad. Many African Americans who lived in Gettysburg worshipped at one time at the local white churches, both the Methodist Church and the United Presbyterian Church. Presbyterian Church records document a baptism of black members as early as 1815. In most "integrated" churches of the North, black worshippers were second-class members, relegated to the balcony or the "African pews" in the back of the church. Gettysburg was no exception. Between 1837 and 1843, therefore, some forty members of Gettysburg's black community worked to form two churches to serve their needs: Asbury Church and the Wesleyan Methodist Episcopal Church. The first pastor of Asbury Church was Reverend J. J. Matthews. Wesleyan Methodist Episcopal Church later became St. Paul's African Methodist Episcopal (AME) Zion Church. In 1840, Thaddeus Stevens offered a house that he owned for use as a black church. The original site of St. Paul's AME Zion Church was what is now the intersection of Breckinridge Street and Long Lane. A wood-frame church was built on this donated land in 1843. Reverend Abraham Cole served as the first pastor.[4]

Several black men and women with connections to St. Paul's AME Zion Church formed the Slave Refuge Society in the year that the church was established. This organization took an active role in aiding escaped slaves seeking freedom in the North. The church building itself may have been used as a station on the Underground Railroad. Word spread of the abolition activists in Gettysburg. The Maryland legislature expressed anxiety about them, passing a law prohibiting black residents of Gettysburg "from passing and repassing through the state subjecting many of our colored friends to inconvenience." By 1860, the church had grown to forty-eight members.[5]

In 1837, a dynamic newcomer to Gettysburg spurred on the religious and educational development of the town's black community. Daniel Alexander Payne, born a free black in Charleston, South Carolina, taught himself a wide range of subjects. He opened his first school in Charleston in 1829, teaching the children of free blacks by day and adult slaves by night. By 1835, sixty students attended his school, including children "from most of the leading families of Charleston." But in December 1834, South Carolina passed a law, to be effective April 1, 1835, making it a crime punishable by fine and whipping to teach any slave or free person of color to read or write.[6]

This legislation forced Payne to travel north, and he was invited to study at the Lutheran Theological Seminary in Gettysburg. He had a huge impact on the black population of Gettysburg during his two years there. No AME church existed in Gettysburg when Payne arrived, so he set out in 1837 to prepare the way for the first. Payne also wanted to stimulate scholarship in the town's black community, conducting classes in a classroom provided by Pennsylvania College (later renamed Gettysburg College). He explained in his autobiography,

> While pursuing my studies at the Seminary I obtained permission to use an old building belonging to the College for Sunday-school instruction. So, gathering in all the colored children in the neighborhood, I opened the school, having for teachers such persons as I could obtain from the village and the Seminary. As occasion did permit I also held religious meetings, and labored to produce revivals, which labors were blessed by the coming of many souls to Christ. I also organized societies among the women for mental and moral improvement.[7]

Payne's rigorous course of studies at the seminary included German, Hebrew, Greek, ecclesiastical history, philosophy, archaeology, and systematic theology. Dr. Samuel S. Schmucker, an ardent abolitionist, became his mentor. The kindly administrator also provided for his student's physical needs, but Payne, feeling a need to help support himself, worked at tasks from cutting wood to cleaning boots. He was ordained as a Lutheran minister in Philadelphia but soon returned to the AME church. He went on to a distinguished career as a religious leader and an advocate for education. He traveled extensively through America and Europe and became a powerful voice against slavery. In 1852, he was ordained a bishop in the AME church and served as president of Wilberforce University until his death in 1893.[8]

Free black children attended school in Gettysburg as early as 1824. The 1834 Pennsylvania Free School Act required communities to establish schools for their children. In response to the act, the town of Gettysburg set up five schools. The town was divided into four geographical sections. In each quadrant, a school for white children was set up. A fifth school was set up for "colored" students. The original school at the corner of South Washington Street and High Street was described as a one-story building, "rudely furnished with home-made desks and benches." Thirty-three children attended this school, 46 percent of those eligible. School attendance was not mandatory at that time, and more children might have attended if they had not been needed to support their families. Indeed, 70 percent of the children from property-owning black families took classes there. A white woman, Elizabeth Keech, served as the first teacher, but in 1839, she was succeeded by a black man, J. Sibbs, and the school was moved to the AME church. A new school would be built 1883–1884.[9]

The economic status of African Americans in Gettysburg differed little from that of blacks living elsewhere in the North. Although they constituted 8 percent of the town's population, they owned less than 1 percent of the total value of either real estate or personal property. The most common occupation for men was "day laborer," while women were most often listed as "domestic servant." African Americans in the town made their living in a wide range of occupations, including cook, hostler, blacksmith, waiter, nurse, clergy, brickmaker, janitor, fortune-teller, shoemaker, teamster, and wagonmaker. Some, such as Owen Robinson, did more than one job or changed jobs with the seasons. Robinson, listed as a "confectioner" in the 1860 census, operated a small restaurant selling oysters in the winter and ice cream in the summer. He also served as sexton of the local Presbyterian church. One way or another, blacks supported themselves; census records show that no blacks lived in the almshouse in 1860.[10]

In 1790, James Gettys and others built a stone gristmill along Rock Creek, just south of Gettysburg. James McAllister, an ardent white abolitionist, bought the mill on May 23, 1827. An antislavery group assembled there on the Fourth of July, 1836, the sixtieth anniversary of the Declaration of Independence. The gathering included a number of free black residents of Adams County. The assembly unanimously adopted fourteen resolutions, beginning with a quotation from St. Paul: "God hath made of *one blood* all nations of men." They voiced their support for the assertion in the Declaration of Independence that "all men are created equal" and are "endowed by their creator with certain unalienable rights, among which are life, *liberty*, and the pursuit of happiness." They resolved, "That, if liberty is the *right* of all men, no human being can be *rightfully* held in slavery."[11]

Finally, they committed themselves to fighting against slavery with the words,

> *Resolved*, That although we may be denounced, for our efforts in the cause of human rights, by office-holding and office seeking politicians, and even by men wearing clerical robes, we will not be "afraid of their terror," but, disregarding their denunciations, we will continue to open our mouths for the dumb, and to plead the cause of the oppressed and of those who have none to help them, humbly believing, that, if we do unto others as we wish that they should do unto us, we shall have the approbation of Him who will render every man, according to his works, and whose approbation will be a full remuneration for the loss of this world's favor.[12]

Not everyone in Gettysburg supported these abolitionist views, however. On December 3, 1836, an antislavery meeting convened at the old courthouse that stood in the town's center square where Baltimore Street intersects Chambersburg Street. The meeting was packed with antiabolitionist partisans who had been spreading fears that antislavery agitation would offend and drive away Southern clients of the town's trade and industry and threaten its prosperity.

James McAllister, chairman of the committee, soon lost control of the meeting to the overwhelming crowd opposed to the abolitionists. Many shouted down the speakers and threw eggs at them. Someone in the mob hurled a dead cat at the head of one of the abolitionist leaders, knocking off his top hat. The mob drove the abolitionists out of the courthouse.

The committee would not be easily intimidated, however, and it reassembled that very night in the Gettysburg Academy classroom of Michael C. Clarkson, who had been named vice chairman just before the rioting began. That night, the committee began writing the constitution for the Adams County Anti-Slavery Society. In the coming years the organization grew stronger, attracting such stalwart members as Thaddeus Stevens, a Gettysburg lawyer who spoke out forcefully against slavery. He also helped found Gettysburg's AME Zion Church, providing a temporary site for worship.[13]

McAllister Mill

The McAllister Mill became an important station on the Underground Railroad. It was ideally located only a day's walk from the border with Maryland, a slave state. Although it was close to a major north-south road, intervening woods and higher ground concealed it from passers-by. Fugitives could take advantage of the mill's proximity to Rock Creek to throw off hounds that followed their trail. A contemporary scholar wrote,

> Once a slave reached the mill, his safety was assured. Pursuing search parties were completely baffled in their efforts to find a fugitive's hiding place. Opposite the mill was a thickly wooded hill with giant trees and scrub pines. On the eastern slope there was a rocky cavern called "Wind Cave." Sometimes runaway slaves hid from their pursuers in the rock cave and adjoining dense virgin forest. The exhausting journey usually covered many miles along an ancient Indian path from Maryland. The twisting and turning, rocky and narrow trail led northward to freedom. Fugitives crossed streams and creeks to eliminate their trail from the bloodhounds that followed.[14]

When they arrived, the fugitives would be concealed in the mill itself. McAllister would shut off the flow of water from the millrace, and the refuge seekers would crawl down the sluiceway, hiding behind the waterwheel in the cog pit. Up to ten people could squeeze into this space. The waterwheel inside the mill hid this chamber from prying eyes, and a heavy door lifted by an overhead pulley further concealed the secret compartment. The McAllisters provided food, clothing, and much-needed rest for the sojourners sheltered there. After a period of recuperation, the McAllisters guided the fugitives to the next "station" on the "railroad."

The strict Fugitive Slave Act, part of the Compromise of 1850, made helping a slave escape from bondage even more perilous. Prison awaited anyone aiding slaves in their escape. Nonetheless, in the eight years following the passage of the act, over two hundred slaves passed through this mill on their way to freedom.[15]

One of the most dramatic episodes in the operation of the Underground Railroad in Adams County occurred in 1849. One cloudy evening, a carriage and its pair of horses appeared through the chilly mist. The carriage and its lathered horses, splattered with mud, showed signs of a rough and tiring journey. Repeatedly, the driver glanced anxiously behind him as he turned off the Baltimore Pike onto a narrow dirt path that ran alongside Rock Creek. As the carriage stopped near a farmhouse, an agent of the Underground Railroad jumped quickly from the vehicle and shouted to the farmer, standing by his fence.

"Quick, a guide to Wolf Hill or this poor man is lost. They are too close behind for me to stay on the turnpike, and I don't know the back route." Before he could finish speaking his pursuers appeared in another carriage less than half a mile down the road, racing toward them. "There they are now!" he screamed.

The farmer, Adam Wert, turned to his nine-year-old son and said, "Jump in, boy, and show him to Jimmy's," referring to Jimmy McAllister's mill. The lad hopped onto the seat alongside the driver. "Drive on, I'll show you," he instructed. The carriage lurched forward, plunging through soggy ditches and through mud halfway to the hubs. The steep hills, the sharp curves, and the closeness of trees to the road intimidated the driver. The boy kept exhorting him to go faster. Soon they could hear the voices of their pursuers, who had closed to within two hundred yards. The frustrated boy grabbed the reigns from the driver and urged the horses ahead at full speed. A wild, jolting ride followed over stumps and tree roots, the carriage's hubs bumping against the trees flanking the trail.

The carriage chasing them fared worse. That speeding vehicle crashed into a rock and tumbled into the creek. Residents of the Gettysburg area would long speak of this as the worst carriage wreck in memory. This mishap gave time for the McAllisters to conceal the fugitive in a "snug rock cave," one of the caverns on Wolf Hill known as the "Wind Caves." After a tense night in hiding, the passenger continued along the railroad, through York Springs and Harrisburg, northward to safety.[16]

When the Civil War came, the hard hand of war tragically touched the McAllisters. On June 26, 1863, five days before the major Gettysburg fighting began, local militia tried their best to delay the approaching Confederates but had to flee before them. Some of the militiamen veered off the Baltimore Pike and tried to cut across McAllister's field for the safety of the thick woods beyond. But the Southerners opened fire on them, knocking a Gettysburg lad, George Washington Sandoe, off his horse. James McAllister ran to give aid to Sandoe but to no avail. He lifted the young man's body into his wagon and brought him home for burial. Sandoe may have been the first to die for the Union at Gettysburg, and he was killed on the grounds of one of the most active Underground Railroad stations.[17]

During the battle, the Union line extended to the mill. After the battle, the mill served as a field hospital. The McAllister family paid a personal price in the war for the Union. All five of James's sons served the cause. One, Theodore, was wounded, captured, and confined in the notorious Georgia prisoner-of-war camp at Andersonville. Another son, James, was killed at Vicksburg, the fortified Confederate city on the Mississippi River, which surrendered to Maj. Gen. Ulysses S. Grant the day after fighting at Gettysburg ended.[18]

Other Underground Railroad Activity

Some believe that the Dobbin House, built by the hands of slaves, may have ironically become a hiding place for escaped slaves. When Reverend Alexander Dobbin died in 1809, his son, Matthew, inherited the house. Matthew lived there until only 1820. After he moved from Gettysburg, Dobbin aided runaway slaves so actively that he was known as a "captain" in the Underground Railroad. No evidence indicates that Dobbin engaged in such activity while living in Gettysburg; however, on a back stairway of the building, an ordinary-looking pantry shelf concealed a secret compartment. Sliding the shelf to the side revealed a hidden crawlspace that, persistent legend claims, was used to secrete fugitives. The credibility of this story is greatly diminished by the fact that Matthew's father, Reverend Dobbin, owned slaves himself.[19]

One of Gettysburg's most active black operatives in the Underground Railroad was Basil Biggs. Biggs did not have an easy life. He was born in Carroll County, Maryland, in 1819, and his mother died when he was only four years old, leaving him $400 to pay for his education. He was "bound out," however, doing hard manual labor for thirteen years, and the money ran out before he could get any schooling. He finally became a teamster, someone who drives the teams of horses on a wagon. Biggs married Mary J. Jackson and began a family. In 1858, just three years before the outbreak of the Civil War, he sold all his property and moved his family to Gettysburg. He was illiterate, but he wanted his children to have an education, which they could not have gotten in Maryland, where teaching blacks to read was forbidden. Here he also operated his own branch of the Underground Railroad. He may have concealed runaway slaves in his home during the day. By night, he would secrete them to Quaker Valley, from which they could continue on their flight to Canada. He probably used either the McPherson Barn or a nearby quarry west of the barn to conceal his "passengers" until it was safe to move to the next station.[20]

At the time of the Battle of Gettysburg, Biggs lived as a tenant at the Crawford Farm along Marsh Creek, near Black Horse Tavern Road west of town. Shortly after the battle, Biggs inherited the farm of John Fisher, who in his will had left him his land and a small log house on Cemetery Ridge. Biggs became a successful farmer and purchased the adjoining Fry Farm. He developed a reputation as a skilled veterinarian; the local people called on him often, many of them referring to him as "Dr. Biggs." He was held in such great respect that when he joined an organization called "The Sons of Good Will," the membership called on him to serve as vice president and as treasurer, even though he remained illiterate.[21]

Margaret Palm was one of the more interesting characters in Gettysburg. Only twenty-seven years old at the time of the battle, she may have been one of the most active agents of the Underground Railroad. Her reputation was such that several attempts were made to seize her and bear her off into slavery. She owned a musket to protect herself and her "passengers." On one occasion, a group of slave owners plotted to kidnap her. They attacked her and succeeded in tying her hands together but were unable to subdue the strong woman who vigorously resisted. According to the story, one of her assailants made the mistake of letting his thumb get too close to her mouth. She bit it off. A local merchant happened by and came to help her. The rescuer was crippled, but he knew how to wield his crutch, and he helped her fight off the attackers. Truth and fiction are difficult to separate with Mag Palm. When Elsie Singmaster penned her 1924 novel *A Boy in Gettysburg*, she based her character "Maggie Bluecoat" on Margaret Palm. Margaret's story may have been embellished over time, but people certainly believed it at the time. A photograph taken of Mag Palm shows her demonstrating how her hands were tied by the would-be kidnappers.[22]

Black citizens of Gettysburg knew well the danger of kidnapping. Legal documents proving free status provided little protection for black men or women from slave catchers driven by visions of a lucrative payoff for their efforts. Catherine Paine, known as Kitty, was emancipated in 1843. Her erstwhile mistress, the widow Mary Maddox, sold her farm and moved to Pennsylvania with her former slaves, including Kitty Paine. Maddox once again formalized Paine's emancipation at the Adams County Courthouse in Gettysburg. In 1845, a nephew of Mrs. Maddox, along with four cohorts, kidnapped Paine and three of her four children, bringing them to Virginia. Paine went to court in Virginia, pleading the case for her freedom. She lost her case, and her fate is unknown.[23]

One writer suggested in 1883 that some of the faculty of the Lutheran Theological Seminary and Pennsylvania College secretly gave aid to fugitives from the South. On the campus of Pennsylvania College, antislavery students formed a secret society, an unofficial fraternity called "The Black Ducks." They constructed a hiding place on Culp's Hill, southwest of town. Near the crest of the hill stood two parallel rocks, five feet apart, ten feet high. They fashioned a roof with heavy corn wood and used earth to cover their handiwork and to seal the open area, except for a well-concealed entrance.[24]

According to one account, the Black Ducks worked in cooperation with Jack Hopkins, the black custodian of Pennsylvania College. The college had hired Hopkins in 1847. He took care of the building and grounds, rang the school bell, kept the fires going in the classrooms, and performed ad hoc assignments, such as erasing graffiti in the halls and private rooms. Hopkins owned a house in Gettysburg's black neighborhood, but after 1860, the school provided him with a home on campus, which stood about where the Musselman Library is now located. He then rented out his house at 219 South Washington Street. Hopkins's reputation extended well beyond Gettysburg. He could apparently organize impressive festivities. A local newspaper recalled a memorable Fourth of July celebration:

> The fireworks, however, were not the grandest feature of Gettysburg's Independence evening, 1860. They were simply nowhere alongside of the "Grand Fancy Dress Ball" given at the residence of John Hopkins, janitor of the College, which was attended by all the colored aristocracy of the town, with specially invited guests from York, Harrisburg, Columbia, and Chambersburg.

The house could not hold the great crowd, and the revelers had to take turns on the dance floor. It is unclear whether the festivities took place in Hopkins's own home on Washington Street or in the house provided by the college. It is also unclear whether Hopkins used his home to conceal escaped slaves. Since aiding a fugitive slave was a felony, the Black Ducks kept no written records, and little information is available about their activities or about Jack Hopkins's possible role. The very existence of the organization is in some dispute.[25]

An old woodcut print of Gettysburg, however, provides a clue to the web that may have connected a number of antislavery agents. Staunch abolitionist Thaddeus Stevens owned an ironworks at Caledonia, west of Gettysburg, and another at Maria Furnace, at the western end of Adams County. Stevens hoped to connect the latter factory with the railroad that came into Gettysburg from the east. Although the railroad bed had been graded and prepared between the ironworks and Gettysburg, the tracks had not been laid, because of lack of funding. Travelers could proceed along the railroad bed, avoiding the main roads. The old woodcut, which shows a wagon traveling along this route with the town of Gettysburg in the distance, bears a notation handwritten by local abolitionist J. Howard Wert:

> Stevens' R.R. used by fugitives
>> From his ironworkes [sic]
>> To Pa. College. Jack
>> Hopkins notified the B.D.'s [Black Ducks]
>> Who took them to Wright's.

This woodcut shows the bed of the unfinished railroad west of Gettysburg. The notation, by J. Howard Wert, indicates that fugitive slaves used this untracked railroad bed as a pathway from Thaddeus Stevens's iron works in Caledonia, Pennsylvania, to Gettysburg. This road skirts the edge of the campus of Pennsylvania College, where Jack Hopkins and the Black Ducks could provide safe passage to the North. Courtesy of the J. Howard Wert Gettysburg Collection.

The Wrights referred to are William and Phebe Wright of York Springs, north of Gettysburg. The Wrights carried a reputation for active participation in the Underground Railroad. On one occasion, slave hunters burst into their house while they were harboring a freedom-seeking family. The adults were effectively concealed, but their baby would not stop crying. Mrs. Wright quickly wrapped up the baby and held the child as her own. The slave hunters, rebuked for disturbing a mother and child, were shamed into leaving. Mrs. Wright later commented that she was glad the men did not get a look at the child.[26]

Notes

1. Robert L. Bloom, A History of Adams County, Pennsylvania 1700–1990 (Gettysburg, PA: Adams County Historical Society [ACHS], 1992), 28–29; Peter C. Vermilyea, "The Effect of the Confederate Invasion of Pennsylvania on Gettysburg's African American Community," The Gettysburg Magazine 24 (January 2001), 112; see also Betty Myers, "History of Blacks in Adams County," audiotape on file at ACHS; Shelley L. Jones and Harry Stokes, Black History in Our Community, privately published (ACHS).

2. Harry Bradshaw Matthews, Whence They Came: Families of United States Colored Troops in Gettysburg, Pennsylvania, 1815–1871 (privately published, 1992), 76, 77, 86; Vermilyea, "The Effect of the Confederate Invasion," 112.

3. Matthews, *Whence They Came*, 76, 77, 86; Harry Bradshaw Matthews, *Revisiting the Battle of Gettysburg: The Presence of African Americans before and after the Conflict* (Oneonta, NY: privately published, 1995), 3.

4. Matthews, *Whence They Came*, 65, 67, 78, 80; Charles H. Glatfelter, *The Churches of Adams County, Pennsylvania: A Brief Review and Summary* (Biglerville, PA: St. Paul's Lutheran Church, 1987); Matthews, *Revisiting the Battle of Gettysburg*, 4.

5. Matthews, *Whence They Came*, 65, 67, 78, 80; Glatfelter, *The Churches of Adams County*; Matthews, *Revisiting the Battle of Gettysburg*, 4.

6. Daniel Alexander Payne, *Recollections of Seventy Years* (Nashville, TN: A. M. E. Sunday School Union, 1888; reprinted, New York: Arno Press, 1969), 19, 25, 27–28; Matthews, *Revisiting the Battle of Gettysburg*, 3.

7. Payne, *Recollections of Seventy Years*, 59.

8. Payne, *Recollections of Seventy Years*, 59–60; Vermilyea, "The Effect of the Confederate Invasion," 114; Matthews, *Whence They Came*, 91, from Gettysburg College, *Trustee Minutes Book 1837*, 39.

9. Matthews, *Whence They Came*, 75; Vermilyea, "The Effect of the Confederate Invasion," 115; "Gettysburg Schools," "Teachers in the Colored Schools," file, ACHS, 1, 1b: Elwood W. Christ, "Pennsylvania History Resource Form for 201 South Washington Street," 1989, ACHS; Gettysburg School Board Minutes, ACHS.

10. Vermilyea, "The Effect of the Confederate Invasion," 113; 1860 U.S. census; Charles McCurdy, *Gettysburg: A Memoir* (Pittsburgh, PA: Reed & Witting, 1929).

11. G. Craig Caba, ed., *Episodes of Gettysburg and the Underground Railroad: As Witnessed and Recorded by Professor J. Howard Wert* (Gettysburg, PA: privately published, 1998), 17–19.

12. Caba, *Episodes of Gettysburg*, 21.

13. Caba, *Episodes of Gettysburg*, 30–31; Matthews, *Whence They Came*, 78, 80.

14. Caba, *Episodes of Gettysburg*, 53.

15. Caba, *Episodes of Gettysburg*, 53–54.

16. Caba, *Episodes of Gettysburg*, 70–72.

17. Caba, *Episodes of Gettysburg*, 55.

18. Caba, *Episodes of Gettysburg*, 54–55.

19. Walter L. Powell, *The Alexander Dobbin House: A Short History* (Gettysburg, PA: privately published, 1989); Vermilyea, "The Effect of the Confederate Invasion," 113; Charles L. Blockson, "Escape from Slavery: The Underground Railroad," *National Geographic* 166, no. 1 (July 1984), 25.

20. Vermilyea, "The Effect of the Confederate Invasion," 113; Obituary, "Basil Biggs," *Gettysburg Compiler*, June 13, 1906, Biggs Family file, No. 1000, ACHS.

21. Matthews, *Whence They Came*, 108; Gettysburg Civilians file, "Basil Biggs," United States Army Military History Institute, Carlisle, PA.

22. Vermilyea, "The Effect of the Confederate Invasion," 115–16; David Schick to Elsie Singmaster, Palm Family file, No. 1000, ACHS; Matthews, *Whence They Came*, 137n.

23. Debra McCauslin, "Kitty Paine's Pain," unpublished paper, 2004, ACHS (Kitty Paine's story has been published elsewhere, but the original research by Debra Sandoe McCauslin has not been credited).

24. Caba, *Episodes of Gettysburg*, 73–76.

25. Charles H. Glatfelter, *A Salutary Influence: Gettysburg College 1832–1985* (Gettysburg, PA: Gettysburg College, 1987), 151–53. Peter C. Vermilyea, "Jack Hopkins' Civil War," *Adams Count History* 11 (2005): 4–21; *Star and Sentinel*, January 30, 1907.

26. Woodcut, J. Howard Wert Gettysburg Collection.

~

CHAPTER TWO

African Americans and the Civil War

War Begins: Blacks Volunteer

With Abraham Lincoln's election, Southern states began to secede. When Southern guns opened fire on the American flag flying at Fort Sumter, the war came. Thousands of blacks volunteered to fight in the Northern armies. For them, it was clearly a war against slave states and, therefore, a war against slavery. Most Northern whites did not see it that way. For them, it was a war to preserve the Union as it was, slavery included. Declaring it to be a "white man's war," the Federal government and its agents turned away black volunteers.

Undeterred, thousands of blacks enlisted in the U.S. Navy, which accepted volunteers irrespective of race. They also found acceptance as workers in the many necessary ancillary services connected with the army, such as the quartermaster, commissary, ordinance, and medical departments.

Teamsters

One of the most essential roles that blacks took on was that of teamster. Thousands of wagons accompanied the Union armies, carrying munitions, food, medical supplies, and other needs. Pay records filed by the quarter-master for the period during the Gettysburg Campaign indicate that the overwhelming majority of the teamsters were African Americans. Indeed, the payroll for the quartermaster station for Frederick, Maryland, right in the center of the campaign's zone of operations, shows twenty-five "Colored

The quartermaster payroll roster from the Frederick, Maryland, station, written at the end of June 1863, reports the Union quartermaster activity for the chronological and geographical epicenter of the Gettysburg campaign. It lists one wagonmaster, one assistant wagonmaster, one teamster, and twenty-five colored teamsters. Detail from quartermaster report dated July 19, 1863.

Teamsters" and only one "Teamster." Clearly, African Americans played a major role in this crucial work.[1]

A recruiting poster from that time demonstrated how much black teamsters were valued. It read,

WANTED IMMEDIATELY

100
Colored Teamsters!
For the Army of the Potomac.
WAGES,
$20 PER MONTH
AND RATIONS.[2]

According to the poster, black teamsters would earn twenty dollars per month. This is double the amount initially paid to black soldiers. It is even more than the monthly pay for white soldiers.

Some might dismiss this role as unimportant, as not difficult or demanding, or as not dangerous, but they would be wrong on all counts. First, teamsters were crucially important. Logistics very often make the difference between success in a military campaign and failure. The army could not be sustained without a constant supply of food, ammunition, medical supplies, and other materials. Wagons made up the "motor pool" of the Civil War. In emergencies, the teamsters were also called on to do tasks beyond their normal routine. At the beginning of the Gettysburg Campaign, the fast-moving Confederates threatened to overrun the Federal garrisons at Winchester and Martinsburg. They would have captured about a thousand government horses, but black laborers and teamsters mounted them and rode off just as the Southern forces closed in. Testimony in a court of inquiry indicated the success of that part of the evacuation: "We did not leave a horse behind fit for service. There were about 1,000 Government horses mounted by teamsters, contrabands, and sick soldiers on the flank."[3]

Second, this was difficult work. Anyone familiar with the phrase "stubborn as a mule" has some idea of the frustrations of trying to get a mule to do what it is supposed to do. One Civil War veteran recalled, "One of our teamsters used to remark that one of his mules wouldn't go unless he did use the whip, another stopped 'right plumb' when struck with one, while still another wouldn't pull a pound unless yelled at in a peculiar manner."

He also recounted the skill of a black teamster:

At one time, when the driver was separated from his team, the black mule was unhappy and refused to be comforted. He did not eat with his

WANTED IMMEDIATELY!
100
Colored Teamsters!
For the Army of the Potomac.
WAGES,
$20 PER MONTH
AND RATIONS.
FRANK PFEIFFER,
Master Mechanic.

U. S. Steam-Power Book and Job Print, Ledger Buildings

Teamster poster. Courtesy of the Library Company of Philadelphia.

accustomed appetite, and kicked viciously at all who approached from the front or rear. The mule at last became so unmanageable that Jim was sent for. Upon his arrival his muleship became quiet, and allowed himself to be harnessed and driven, with a humility quite touching to those who had seen him in his refractory mood.[4]

One observer commented on the importance of teamsters and the demanding nature of their work:

> In the Army of the Potomac there are probably 8,000–10,000 negroes employed as teamsters. This is a business they are well fitted for, and, of course, it relieves and equal number of white men for other duties. A teamster's life is a very hard one particularly at this season of the year. It does not matter how much it storms, or how deep the mud, subsistence must be hauled to the camps, day and night, taking along with tired horses and mules. The creaking wagons are kept busy carrying to and from commissary, quartermaster and ordnance stores, in addition to keeping the camps supplied with fire-wood.[5]

Third, it was very dangerous work. The Confederate Congress declared that any black man in the uniform of the United States would be considered to be aiding in the freeing of slaves and therefore taking part in a slave insurrection. The Confederates' government declared that it would send into slavery or execute any such soldiers if captured. Black teamsters in the Union army also took part in military operations. While Confederates who captured white teamsters would usually treat them as prisoners of war, they did not necessarily extend the same courtesy to black teamsters. Not protected by rules of war, black teamsters might well experience brutal treatment. A month before the Gettysburg Campaign, Maj. Gen. David Hunter complained in a letter to President Lincoln, "Many colored teamsters, laborers and servants employed by the army when captured by the enemy have been sold into slavery."[6]

Many other reports in the official records indicate the hardship and danger that the drivers faced. Col. J. B. Rogers reported laconically, "Very cold. Thirteen teamsters frozen on our forage train." Capt. James I. Powell described an attack on his teamsters: "At the moment of the attack the rear guard gave way and the rebels seeing this dashed upon the wagons, firing at teamsters and mules." Several accounts of operations in the Western campaigns describe outright murder, such as this report: "6 teamsters are known to be killed, 2 soldiers and 1 teamster were wounded and 4 soldiers are still unaccounted for. The indications are that these men were wounded and killed from pure maliciousness and after they had surrendered."[7]

A Union cavalry officer reported a similar incident:

> Outnumbered and overpowered at last they had to abandon the six wagons for which they had fought, leaving besides in the hands of the enemy 3 prisoners, who have since returned paroled. The 6 colored teamsters were butchered without mercy and the wagons destroyed.[8]

These examples indicate the perils faced by black Union teamsters. The thousands of black teamsters of the U.S. Army performed a difficult, skilled, and important function. They also carried out their responsibilities in spite of grave personal danger.

During the Gettysburg Campaign, a Union supply wagon train traveled toward Rockville, Maryland, not far from the nation's capital. A newspaper reporter described what happened:

> By the time we reached our first post of cavalry pickets we came up with the rear of a long wagon train, comprising one hundred and fifty vehicles, each drawn by six mules, driven by a very black and picturesque Negro. This train must have been at least two miles long.[9]

As this wagon train came to within two miles of Rockville, an excited rider from that direction warned the caravan of hundreds of Rebel cavalry just ahead. The mule teams halted, and the drivers desperately tried to turn the wagons around. Teams tangled together in a massive traffic jam, with some of the wagons overturning in their attempts to reverse direction. In the midst of this panic and confusion, the Southern cavalry of Lt. Gen. J. E. B. Stuart suddenly appeared and fell upon their prey.

Supply Train, *by Edwin Forbes. Courtesy of the Library of Congress.*

One of Stuart's staff officers, W. W. Blackford, described the scene:

Galloping full tilt into the head of the train, we captured a small guard and a lot of gaily dressed quartermasters, and over half the wagons, before they could turn round; but then those beyond took the alarm, turned and fled as fast as their splendid mule teams could go. After them we flew, popping away with our pistols at such drivers as did not pull up, but the more we popped, the faster those in front plied the whip; finally, coming to a sharp turn in the road, one upset and a dozen or two others piled up on top of it. . . . All behind this blockade were effectually stopped, but half a dozen wagons had made the turn before this happened and after them two or three of us dashed. . . . When the last was taken I found myself on a hill in full view of Washington. One hundred and twenty-five uninjured wagons were taken and safely brought into our lines, together with the animals of the others.[10]

The Confederates captured nearly all of these teamsters. Two of them escaped, one of them wounded. Actually, the Confederate seizure of these wagons may have had an important *positive* impact on the Gettysburg Campaign for the Union. Stuart's men wasted precious time writing paroles for their four hundred Union prisoners and procuring their signatures. Douglas Southall Freeman would state, "This wagon train was 'Jeb's' stumbling block." The cavalry commander fatefully decided that "a captured train of '125 best United States model wagons and splendid teams with gay caparisons'—this must be brought back to Virginia, no matter where, meantime, it had to be carried." The captured wagons slowed down the movement of Stuart's command and contributed to his delay in rejoining the main part of Lee's army. Stuart's absence left the Confederate commander without the military intelligence that he needed while moving through hostile territory. Lee was forced to plan and fight the first two days of the great three-day battle without the help of his cavalry commander.[11]

African Americans Become Soldiers

In July 1862, the U.S. Congress overhauled the seventy-year-old Militia Act, changing the section that excluded blacks and empowering President Lincoln to organize and employ African Americans "for any military or naval service for which they be found competent." Lincoln's Emancipation Proclamation, which took effect on January 1, 1863, formally authorized the organization and participation of African Americans as soldiers in the army of United States.

Even before Lincoln's proclamation, Union military leaders had already employed the "sable arm" that Frederick Douglass had been urging the government to use. In 1862, in the Union-occupied coastal region of South Carolina, Maj. Gen. David Hunter assembled former slaves into a unit of soldiers, uniformed and armed. This unit became the vanguard for the First South Carolina Infantry (African Descent), the first Union regiment of African American troops in the Civil War. Eventually the command of the regiment came to Col. Thomas Wentworth Higginson, who had given financial and moral support to John Brown. Higginson's *Army Life in the Black Regiment* would become a classic of Civil War literature.[12]

James H. Lane, Kansas senator and general of his state's militia, organized the First Regiment of the Kansas Colored Infantry. This unit fought the first engagement and suffered the first combat deaths of any black regiment when it clashed with Confederates on October 29, 1862, at Island Mound, Missouri. Even before the Gettysburg Campaign began, the First Kansas fought Confederate forces at Sherwood on May 18 and at Bush Creek on May 2, also in Missouri. On July 2, 1863, while fighting raged at Gettysburg in the Wheatfield, the Peach Orchard, Devil's Den, and on Little Round Top, the First Kansas fought a Confederate force of Texans and their American Indian allies in the Battle of Cabin Creek, in the Cherokee Nation territory that would one day become the state of Oklahoma.[13]

One of the most unusual arrangements of the war concerned black volunteers in New Orleans. Free blacks as well as slaves had fought in defense of that city as early as 1727, when the French controlled the area. When the Spanish took over, local blacks fought for them. They even aided the American Revolution by helping in the capture of British-controlled Pensacola. After Louisiana became part of the United States, free black men of the area remained in the service of the state of Louisiana. Black soldiers also joined Andrew Jackson and fought to defend New Orleans in the War of 1812. With this long history of loyal service, it is not surprising that the state of Louisiana, upon seceding from the Union, accepted the enlistment of free black men. "The Louisiana Native Guard" included black officers as well as enlisted men.[14]

When New Orleans fell to Federal forces early in the war, the Native Guard was ordered to evacuate the city along with the rest of the Confederate defenders. The black soldiers did not follow these orders. Maj. Gen. Benjamin Butler of Massachusetts took charge in New Orleans. Earlier in the war, this general, while in command at Fort Monroe, had found a loophole by which he could circumvent the Fugitive Slave Law. When Confederate officers, under a flag of truce, requested the return of slaves who had fled to the Union lines, Butler claimed the fugitives as "contraband of war." This set a precedent. From then on, Union officers could refuse to return fugitives, and the word *contraband* came to be synonymous with blacks from the South.

In New Orleans, Butler again used his legal acumen to find a novel way around government restriction against enlisting blacks. The government had recently announced that former Confederate soldiers who swore an oath of allegiance to the United States could be enlisted in the Union forces. Since this directive did not specify race, Butler officially directed on August 22, 1862, nearly a year before Gettysburg, that these black "former Confederates" be enlisted in the volunteer service of the United States. As the Gettysburg Campaign unfolded in the East, these troops, now designated the Corps d'Afrique, attacked and besieged Port Hudson, a Confederate stronghold on the Mississippi River. The fort capitulated on July 9, 1863, six days after "Pickett's Charge" climaxed the Battle of Gettysburg.[15]

At Milliken's Bend, Louisiana, on June 7, 1863, supported by a white regiment and the fire of two gunboats, another new unit of black recruits, inexperienced in battle, repelled a series of vicious attacks by veteran Confederates. Thus, while the Army of the Potomac and the Army of Northern Virginia struggled through the Gettysburg Campaign, thousands of African Americans were battling in other theaters, from the Carolina coast to the Mississippi and beyond.[16]

Black Confederates

On the Confederate side, Southern blacks were not only important but *essential* to the war effort. This should be no surprise. In fact, of the Confederate population of about nine million, three and a half million were slaves and a quarter million were free blacks. Blacks, making up nearly four million of the nine million people in the South, represented by necessity an important part of nearly every Southern undertaking, not just agriculture but also industry, commerce, transportation, construction, even music and art. They were excluded from participating in some areas, such as education, but were key contributors in nearly all others.

Every army reflects the society from which it comes. No one in the South thought for a minute that the Confederacy would carry on the war without the active and extensive participation of its black population. Blacks made up most of the teamsters, laborers, cooks, and officers' servants who accompanied the Confederate army to Gettysburg. One historian estimates that ten thousand black teamsters drove the wagons of Lee's army through the Pennsylvania campaign and that another ten thousand blacks accompanied the army in other capacities.

Blacks performed crucial functions on the home front as well. They took on major roles in moving supplies, providing medical services, and carrying out every essential part of noncombat service. They made up most of the staff at military hospitals, such as the massive Chimborazo Hospital complex in Richmond. They made up most of the labor force at Tredegar Iron Works, which manufactured cannon for the Southern armies and fashioned the iron plating for the famous ironclad ship CSS *Virginia* (originally the USS *Merrimack*). Blacks dug the entrenchments, drove the wagons, and did every other kind of ancillary service that an army needed in order to function in the field.[17]

So, it should not be surprising that observers North and South pointed out that as the Southern armies marched by, as much as one quarter of the forces appeared to be black. It may arouse controversy, but it would be difficult to refute the argument that without the continued contribution of Southern blacks to its war effort, the Confederacy could probably not have continued organized resistance past the summer of 1863. It certainly could not have launched the offensive operation that carried the war into Pennsylvania in July 1863. In other words, without the contributions of African Americans to the Southern war effort, there would not have been—could not have been— a Battle of Gettysburg.

The most controversial aspect of this whole subject may be the African Americans who served as soldiers in the Confederate army. This issue has become hopelessly politicized. On the one side are those, especially African Americans, who argue that no blacks would ever voluntarily serve in a war to preserve slavery. They argue that if any blacks served in the Confederate army, they did so only because they were coerced and would escape at the first good opportunity.

On the other side of the argument are those who argue that the Civil War was not about slavery, that slavery had nothing to do with Southern motives. They support their argument by claiming that the blacks of the South rose up in concert with whites to fight for Southern rights. Part of their evidence is that thousands of blacks actively served in the Confederate armies. There is extensive anecdotal evidence of free blacks and slaves who served devotedly—the slaves loyally serving their masters and the free men apparently volunteering of their own free will. The motives of these men, like all human motives, are complex and should not be oversimplified. Blacks had defended their homes from "invaders" throughout history. Northerners could have been viewed as just another invading army, particularly at the beginning of the conflict when ending slavery was not part of the Northern rationale for war.

But were the African Americans accompanying the Confederate army actually combat soldiers? One should remember that just traveling along with an army and wearing a soldier's cap, even toting a weapon, does not make someone a soldier. In fact, throughout the South, strong antipathy against this practice led to laws prohibiting blacks from carrying any kind of weapon; it is unlikely that this aversion would vanish with the outbreak of war. Furthermore, the Confederate government specifically prohibited the enlistment of African Americans, and it continued this prohibition right up until the last weeks of the war. Even then, the enlisting of blacks was approved only after a plea by Robert E. Lee himself. A large minority still heatedly opposed the move, stating that making African Americans soldiers would be against everything for which they were fighting. Why would the Confederate Congress hotly debate implementing a policy that was already practiced extensively?

One eyewitness to the Antietam Campaign estimated that over three thousand blacks accompanied the Confederate army:

> They had arms, rifles, muskets, sabers, bowie-knives, dirks, etc. They were supplied, in many instances, with knapsacks, haversacks, canteens, etc., and they were manifestly an integral portion of the Southern Confederacy army. They were seen riding on horses and mules, driving wagons, riding on caissons, in ambulances, with the staff of generals and promiscuously mixed up with all the Rebel horde.

The observer states that "in many instances" they had knapsacks, haversacks, and canteens, but he does not say that they carried arms "in many instances." This leaves it unclear how many were actually bearing weapons. In any case, a person assigned to haul weapons on a long march will not necessarily be using them in battle.

Many have quoted an account in the *New York Herald* of July 24, 1863, stating, "Among the rebel prisoners who were marched through Gettysburg there were observed seven negroes in uniform and fully accoutred as soldiers." Since these men were all prisoners, they would not have been *fully* accoutred, since their weapons would have been taken away. Without weapons, there would have been little in the way of accoutrements by which to differentiate between soldiers and noncombatants.[18]

Anecdotal evidence abounds to support the loyalty of Southern blacks. Veterans told many stories of black servants seeking out their wounded companions or masters and helping them back for medical treatment or in some cases retrieving their dead bodies or bringing home the surviving horses of deceased masters. There are also cases of Southern blacks captured along with their white compatriots who went with them to prisoner-of-war camps, even when offered the opportunity to walk away in freedom. This action by captured blacks happened too often to be ignored but not enough to be held up as the standard.[19]

Difficult to believe as it may be, some free blacks actually did volunteer to fight for the Confederacy. One might ask why any black man would fight for a country that treated people of his race so horribly. But one could also ask why during World War I and II, when lynching, segregation, and denial of voting rights were a way of life for Southern blacks, thousands of African Americans volunteered to defend the nation where that happened. Human motivation is complex. Blacks who supported the South expressed a hope that, because of their actions, life would be better for them after the war, that they might gain the respect of the community, or that their children might one day stand as the equals of any other person.

An entire book could be written about Southern blacks who served in the Army of Northern Virginia at Gettysburg, although accurate statistics on overall black participation in the Confederate army are elusive. Blacks who served in Southern armies are listed on the rolls as "Negro man" or "Col'd man." Their actual combat role is doubtful, however, because official records commonly designate them as "musician" or "drummer." Military rank is never to be found. In spite of overwhelming evidence to the contrary, some still insist that black volunteers made up a large part of the Confederate combat force. In fact, the enlistment of slaves was expressly forbidden by the Confederate government throughout the war. The Confederate Congress relented reluctantly after a bitter fight, only a few weeks before Lee surrendered his army. One black man, George Grimes of Caroline County Virginia, enlisted in the famed Marye's Battery of the Fredericksburg Artillery in 1862. This battery fired the first Confederate cannon shot of the Battle of Gettysburg. This soldier had no part in firing that shot, however, because he deserted before the battle. When he was taken into custody, he was court-martialed for desertion. According to the record, however, all charges were dropped because he was found to be a Negro. Clearly, he could not have committed desertion because he was forbidden to join in the first place.

An examination of the life of a single free black man may be useful. The story of Charles F. Lutz could represent those of the unknown numbers of Confederate blacks who fought at Gettysburg. Lutz obviously "passed" as white, as there is no indication in his service record that he is "Negro" or "Colored."[20]

Charles F. Lutz of Opelousas, Louisiana, enlisted for twelve months service on June 23, 1861, at Camp Moore. A tanner by trade, Lutz was single and twenty years of age when he enlisted in the Opelousas Guard Company, which became Company F of the Eighth Louisiana Regiment. He came down with "rhumatism" and was admitted to Chimborazo Hospital No. 5 at Richmond, Virginia, on April 21, 1862; he was transferred in May to Camp

Winder. Lutz reenlisted and, according to Confederate records, received a bounty, a cash bonus for enlisting. (Louisiana, as we have seen, showed unusual tolerance toward blacks in the military, even fielding all-black volunteer units with black officers.)

Lutz served on active duty at many of the major early engagements, including First Manassas (Bull Run), Gaines's Mill, and Fredericksburg. During the Chancellorsville campaign in May 1863, he fought in the heights above Fredericksburg and went "missing falling back from Maryes Hill, 3 May inst." Union forces captured him on May 3 and paroled him. He returned to his unit in time to participate in the "Second Battle of Winchester," at the outset of the Gettysburg Campaign.

At Gettysburg on July 2, as dusk settled in, Lutz's regiment, part of Hays' Brigade, surged forward toward the Union position on East Cemetery Hill. Exposed to severe artillery and rifle fire, the regiment took heavy casualties. It crossed the valley between the hostile lines, climbed the hill under fire, and captured some of the Federal cannon. Lutz took a severe wound in his arm. A Federal counterattack drove him and the rest of his brigade back to their original position. Lutz was among those too seriously wounded to travel South after the battle, and on July 5, Union troops again took him prisoner. His personal service records at one place indicate that he was wounded twice, but they mention no injury other than the single arm wound.

Because of his severe wound, he was sent on July 17 to De Camp General Hospital on David's Island in New York Harbor. Returned again to the South, he was furloughed for thirty days and sent to Episcopal Church Hospital in Williamsburg, Virginia, for treatment of his arm. The army sent him home to recover, but he somehow lost his other arm to amputation in 1864. He did not return, and his name was dropped from the company rolls. A surgeon's certificate of disability discharged him on May 9, 1865, a month after Appomattox. This loyal soldier of the Confederacy applied for a Confederate pension from the state of Louisiana and eventually received it in 1900.[21]

Notes

1. National Archives, RG 92, records of Quartermaster Department, entry 238: "Reports of Persons and Articles Hired (Oversize File) 1863, Capt. John McHarg, Frederick, MD, Vol. II, Report of Deceased & Discharged with Salary Due (July–Dec), Report Dated 19 July 1863."

2. Library Company of Philadelphia.

3. *The War of the Rebellion: A Compilation of the Official Records of the Union and Confederate Armies* (Washington, DC: Government Printing Office, 1880–1891), 1st ser., vol. 72, part 2, 93, 130–31 (hereafter cited as OR).

4. Warren Lee Goss, *Recollections of a Private: A Story of the Army of the Potomac* (New York: Crowell, 1890), 168.

5. William A. Gladstone, *Men of Color* (Gettysburg, PA: Thomas, 1993), 137, from artist, Alfred Waud, commenting on his illustration of teamsters receiving pay, *Harper's Weekly*, March 7, 1863.

6. Major General D. Hunter to A. Lincoln, OR, 2nd ser., vol. 5, 712.

7. OR, 1st ser., vol. 34, pt. 2, 34; vol. 41, pt. 1, 273; vol. 19, 347.

8. OR, 1st ser., vol. 34, pt. 1, 890.

9. "REBEL ATTACK NEAR ROCKVILLE, MD., Washington, D.C., June 29, 1863," in *Rebellion Record: A Diary of American Events, with Narratives, Illustrative Incidents, Poetry, Etc.*, ed. Frank Moore (New York: Putnam, 1861–1866), vol. 7, doc. 83, 325–26.

10. W. W. Blackford, *War Years with Jeb Stuart* (New York: Scribner's, 1946), 224–27, from Earl Schenek Miers and Richard A. Brown, eds., *Gettysburg*, new rev. ed. (New York: Collier Books 1962), 32–33.

11. Cowan to Major Eckert, June 28, 1863, OR, 1st ser., vol. 27, pt. 3, 382.

12. OR, 1st ser., vol. 6, 264; Dudley T. Cornish, *The Sable Arm: Negro Troops in the Union Army* (New York: Longmans Green, 1956; Lawrence: University Press of Kansas, 1987), 32; Thomas Wentworth Higginson, *Army Life in a Black Regiment* (Boston: Houghton Mifflin, 1870); Noah Andre Trudeau, *Like Men of War: Black Troops in the Civil War, 1862–1865* (Boston: Little, Brown, 1998), 15–16; Gladstone, *Men of Color*, 7–10.

13. Cornish, *The Sable Arm*, 69–73; Trudeau, *Like Men of War*, 3–7, 13–14; Gladstone, *Men of Color*, 15–16.

14. Glasdstone, *Men of Color*, 12.

15. OR, 3rd ser., vol. 2, 436–37; Cornish, *The Sable Arm*, 66; Trudeau, *Like Men of War*, 23–46; Gladstone, *Men of Color*, 12–13.

16. Cornish, *The Sable Arm*, 144–45; Trudeau, *Like Men of War*, 46–59.

17. Ervin L. Jordan Jr., *Black Confederates and Afro-Yankees in Civil War Virginia* (Charlottesville, VA: University Press of Virginia, 1995), chaps. 1 and 2; James H. Brewer, *The Confederate Negro* (Durham, NC: Duke University Press, 1969).

18. Isaac W. Heysinger, *Antietam and the Maryland and Virginia Campaigns of 1862* (New York: Neale, 1912), 122; Richard Rollins, "Black Confederates at Gettysburg," *Gettysburg Magazine*, 6 (January 1992): 94–98, 95, also published in Richard Rollins, ed., *Black Southerners in Gray: Essays on Afro-Americans in Confederate* (Armies Redondo Beach, CA: Rank and File, 1994), 129–41.

19. Jordan, *Black Confederates*, 232–51.

20. Jordan, *Black Confederates*, 271; roster from Robert K, Krick, *The Fredericksburg Artillery* (Lynchburg, VA: Howard, 1986). See individual service records, National Archives, examples: Charles F. Lutz, Private, Co. F, 8th LA; James Young, Private, Co. K, 29th Alabama; William Colen Revels, Private, 21st NC; see also Rollins, *Black Southerners in Gray*, 94–98; for a critique of the claim of black Confederates, see Bruce Levine, "In Search of a Usable Past: Neo-confederates and Black

Confederates," in *Slavery and Public History: The Tough Stuff of American Memory*, ed. James Oliver Horton and Lois E. Horton (Chapel Hill: University of North Carolina Press), 187–211.

21. Individual service record, Charles F. Lutz; Arthur W. Bergeron Jr., "Free Men of Color Fought for South," *Washington Times*, January/February 1993, File V8-276, National Park Service Library, Gettysburg, PA; Arthur W. Bergeron Jr., "Louisiana's Free Men of Color," in Rollins, *Black Southerners in Gray*, 37–55.

CHAPTER THREE

~

The Great Rebel Invasion

Pennsylvania Blacks Flee a Mass Kidnapping

Terror spread through the black communities in southern Pennsylvania when they heard of the approaching Confederate army. Whether freeborn or formerly enslaved, African Americans had much to fear. Jacob Hoke described the actions of the invading army around Chambersburg:

> One of the revolting features of this day was the scouring of the fields about the town and searching of houses in portions of the place for Negroes. These poor creatures—those of them who had not fled upon the approach of the foe— sought concealment in the growing wheat fields about the town. Into these the cavalrymen rode in search of their prey, and many were caught—some after a desperate chase and being fired at. In two cases, through the intercession of a friend who had influence with [Confederate General] Jenkins, I succeeded in effecting the release of the captured persons.[1]

Many other witnesses recorded this practice. The Reverend Dr. Philip Schaff observed, "The town was occupied by an independent guerilla band of cavalry, who steal horses, cattle, sheep, store-goods, Negroes and whatever else they can make use of without ceremony and in evident violation of Lee's proclamation read yesterday." He continued,

> On Friday this guerilla band came to town on a regular slave-hunt, which presented the worst spectacle I ever saw in this war. They proclaimed, first, that they would burn down every house which harbored a fugitive slave, and did

not deliver him up within twenty minutes. And then commenced the search upon all the houses upon which suspicion rested. It was a rainy afternoon. They succeeded in capturing several contrabands, among them a woman with two children. A most pitiful sight, sufficient to settle the slavery question for every humane mind.[2]

The next day, June 27, Schaff reported that the Rebel troops drove

twenty-one negroes through town and towards Greencastle or Hagerstown. It was a sight as sad and mournful as the slave-hunt of yesterday. They claimed all these Negroes as Virginia slaves, but I was positively assured that two or three were born and raised in this neighborhood. One, Sam Brooks, split many a cord of wood for me. There were among them women and young children, sitting with sad countenances on the stolen Store-boxes. I asked one of the riders guarding the wagons; "Do you not feel bad and mean in such an occupation?" He boldly replied that "he felt very comfortable. Comfortable. They were only reclaiming their property which we had stolen and harbored."[3]

Rachel Cormany watched the Confederates:

hunting up the contrabands & driving them off by droves. O! How it grated on our hearts to have to sit quietly & look at such brutal deeds—I saw no men among the contrabands—all women & children. Some of the colored people who were raised here were taken along—I sat on the front step as they were driven by just like we would drive cattle. Some laughed & seemed not to care—but nearly all hung their heads. One woman was pleading wonderfully with her driver for her children—but all the sympathy she received from him was a rough "March along"—at which she would quicken her pace again. It is a query what they want with those little babies—whole families were taken. Of course when the mother was taken she would take her children.[4]

The Reverend Thomas Creigh recorded in his diary for Friday, June 26, "A terrible day. The guerillas passing and repassing, one of the saddest of sights, several of our colored persons with them, to be sold into slavery, John Philkill and Findlay Cuff." The Rebels announced that they intended "to search all houses for contrabands and fire arms and that wherever they discovered either they will set fire to the house in which they may be found." The next day he reported that the soldiers left, "taking with them about a dozen colored persons, mostly contrabands, women and children."[5]

The raiders carried many of the "contraband" away in wagons. "Some of the men were bound with ropes, and the children were mounted in front or behind the rebels on their horses." Another citizen observed, "They took all

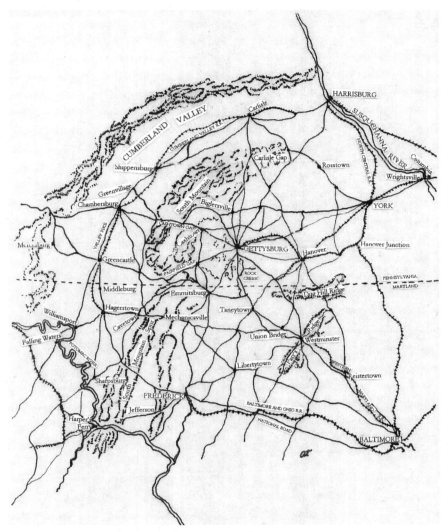

The Gettysburg Campaign. Courtesy of Arleen Thompson.

they could find, even little children, whom they had to carry on horseback before them." William Heyser recorded in his diary on June 18, "The Rebels have left Chambersburg taking with them about 250 colored people again into bondage."[6]

Alarm spread through the town of Gettysburg as well. On Monday, June 15, word of the Confederate capture of Chambersburg reached that town. Salome Myers wrote in her diary that that night the blacks in town "made such a racket up and down by our house that we could not sleep." She later recalled the fear of Gettysburg's black inhabitants:

> Their fear of the rebels was caused by the belief that they would be captured and sold as slaves if the Rebels came north into the States. I know not how much cause they had for their fears, but it was a terrible reality to them. All who could got away and those who were obliged to stay at home were at the shortest notice suddenly transformed into limping, halting, and apparently worthless specimens of humanity.[7]

Tillie Pierce remembered the flight of her town's black population:

> They regarded the rebels as having an especial hatred toward them and they believed that if they fell into their hands, annihilation was sure. These folks mostly lived in the southwestern part of town, and their flight was invariably down Breckinridge Street and Baltimore Street and toward the woods on and around Culp's Hill. I can see them yet: men and women with bundles as large as old-fashioned feather ticks slung across their backs, almost bearing them to the ground. Children also, carrying their bundles, and striving in vain to keep up with their seniors. The greatest consternation was depicted on all their countenances as they hurried along; crowding, and running against each other in their confusion; children stumbling, falling and crying.[8]

Another young Gettysburg resident observed,

> Today we saw Aunt Beckie. She is the colored lady who helps mother with the wash. Jennie and I love Aunt Beckie. She and some other colored people were pulling wagons or pushing wheel barrows and carrying big bundles. . . . "Yo ol' Aunt Beckie is goin' up into de hills. No rebel is gonna catch me and carry me back to be a slave again."[9]

Refugees from Franklin, Adams, and York counties fled in many directions seeking a multitude of safe havens. Many simply flew to the apparent safety of the mountains. Some of Gettysburg's refugees headed for Philadelphia; more fled to Harrisburg; and many fled to the "Golden Hills." This name may refer to Yellow Hill, a small black community seven miles north of the town. The AME Zion Church in that community had stayed in contact with black worshippers in Gettysburg, even sharing preachers. This location would have provided a good hiding place. It was out of the way of major roads and hidden by woods.[10]

Many blacks had fled Gettysburg at the approach of a Confederate force that passed through Gettysburg on the twenty-sixth of June. Some who waited out this passing nightmare decided not to stay for any subsequent intruders. The wife of the Reverend Abraham Cole decided to wait out the Confederate incursion by spending the night with her daughter at Mary Fastnacht's house, hiding in the loft above the kitchen. The anxiety of waiting to be discovered must have been more than what Mrs. Cole could bear. The next day, no sooner had the Southern soldiers left than she and her daughter fled to parts unknown.[11]

Some waited till the last minute to flee. A servant of Fanny Buehler, probably Elizabeth Butler, remained at her employer's house until the Rebel army marched into town. She could bring herself to stay no longer and ran off. Basil Biggs did not make his escape until Confederates had reached the town square on the afternoon of the first day's battle. As the Confederates spilled into town by Chambersburg and Carlisle roads, Biggs, on a borrowed horse, raced out of town down York Road.[12]

Whites remaining in Gettysburg found that much of the labor force that they had come to depend on was gone. Several women in the town would have to take on all the burdens of the household chores. With Jack Hopkins gone, someone else would have to take on the responsibility of ringing the college's bell. The professors met to decide who would take on the chore of the absent black employee. They passed the job on to a temporary tutor.[13]

Some escape stories sound almost too dramatic to be true. Albertus Mc-Creary told the story of "Old Liz," who was probably Elizabeth Butler, a laundress for the McCrearies. McCreary describes the plight of the town's blacks as the Confederates occupied the town:

> On the first day a great many of them were gathered together and marched out of town. As they passed our house our old washerwoman called out "Goodbye, we are going back to slavery." Most of them were crying or moaning. We never expected to see "Old Liz" again, but the day after the battle ended she came walking in, exclaiming, "Thank God, I's alive again!"

She had made her escape by taking advantage of the chaos in town. Her captors marched her and the other prisoners up to Chambersburg Street. With the large crowd milling in the street and with the confusion of the moment, no one saw her slip into the Lutheran Church. She climbed the stairs into the belfry, where she stayed hidden for two days without food or water.[14]

Two historical inconsistencies in this story raise questions of its accuracy. It could only be true if it had occurred during the brief occupation of the town a few days before the battle by Confederates under Jubal Early. If Butler's capture occurred on July 1, the first day of the battle, she would have had to remain hidden, without water, until late on July 4. Severe dehydration would have set in by that time. Another problem with this version is that Confederates extensively used church steeples, attics, and rooftops as observation posts and sniper roosts during the battle. The belfry would be an unlikely choice for a successful hiding place.

A report in the black newspaper *Anglo-African*, however, gives some crecibility to the story by describing a similar escape:

> The people of the town were, to a single instance, moved to sympathy for the unfortunates. The ladies congregated in the church, and having a good hiding place there, they, at given signals, had nearly all of them smuggled into the church. The Rebel guards were puzzled and enraged as the number of their prisoners steadily decreased. The crowds of men and women around them condoled with them in their discomfits, and at the same time kept passing the prisoners into the church.
>
> We must pay tribute to the courage and loyalty of the ladies of Gettysburg. Mrs. Harris kept her hiding place three days. During that time she was in hiding distance of the rebel pickets. . . . Those of the party that found their way into the church escaped, but large numbers were sent to the rebel rear, thence to the land of slavery.[15]

According to another story, Jack, a black farmhand, was unable to run from the Rebels, and so he crawled under a haystack and went three or four days without eating. What makes the last story particularly hard to believe is that any haystack large enough to hide a man would have been snatched up quickly to feed some of the many thousands of very hungry horses converging on the town.[16]

Isaac Smith gathered horses together, loaded a wagon with food, and trekked down an old road deep into the woods. He hid there, taking care of the horses and fearing that at any moment the Rebels would discover his hiding place. His employer's sons would come and go to bring him "something to eat and make sure everything was alright."[17]

Other white neighbors would take an even more active role in protecting their black friends. Jacob Taughinbaugh recalled,

> My mother had two Negro servants. We were sure if the Confederates found them they would be taken away. Our front porch was a few feet above the ground, and at one end there was an excavation below ground where you could get the cellar from the outside. This entranceway was separated from the rest of the space under the porch by a wall made of stones without mortar. My mother took away stones enough to let the servants crawl through, then put

the stones back just as they had been. She had to take out a good many stones, too, because one of the Negroes was a great big woman. Someone had to keep a sharp lookout all the time, and as soon as a soldier was seen coming Mother would take the servants down and stow them away. Sometimes there would be men hanging around the house all day. The best she could do then was to take down some food and slip it to them through the space of one stone when none of the men was near about.[18]

A woman identified only as "The Colored Servantmaid" (probably the wife of Isaac Smith) received protection from an unexpected source. She related her story:

We got down into the cellar, and I crawled way back in the darkest corner and piled everything in front of me. I was the only colored person there, and I didn't know what might happen to me. Up in the kitchen was a sick officer, and he wanted the women to come up out of the cellar to take care of him and do some cooking, and he promised they should be well treated. Mr. Hankey says to him, "Would you see a colored person protected if she was to help with the work here?"

He said he would, and he sent out a written somethin' or 'nother orderin' the men to keep out of the kitchen, and he had the door boarded up half way so they could hand in things to be cooked and we could hand 'em out afterward. No one could go out and no one could come in.[19]

On some occasions, captives were freed by the intervention of sympathetic white neighbors. A well-known Chambersburg theologian, the Reverend Dr. Benjamin Schneck, appealed directly to General Albert G. Jenkins for Esque Hall, a "well and favorably known colored man," who had been taken. After convincing the general that the man was no fugitive slave but a longtime resident of the town, Jenkins released Hall. The reverend also obtained the release of two African American employees of the Cumberland Valley Railroad.

Most interventions were probably not so successful. Jemima K. Cree received reports of seizing blacks with alarm, especially when she heard that "Mag," someone she knew personally, numbered among those taken. She rushed to the courthouse where "there were about 25 women and Children, with Mag and Fannie. I interceded for Mag, told them she was free born, etc. The man said he could do nothing, he was acting according to orders. As they were just ready to start, I had to leave; if I could have had time to have seen the General, I might have got her off. Fannie being contraband, we could do nothing about her."[20]

In at least one instance, the rescuers used force. One resident recounted, "In some cases, the Negroes were rescued from the guards. Squire Kaufman and Tom Pauling did this and if they had been caught, the rebels would have killed them."

On June 16 a lightly guarded Confederate wagon caravan passed through Greencastle, twenty-five miles southwest of Gettysburg. The wagons contained thirty or forty black women and children taken from Chambersburg. Suddenly, a group of townspeople surprised the Confederate chaplain and four soldiers guarding the train. They disarmed the Southerners and locked them up in the local jail. They set the captives free. Fearing reprisals against the town, the citizens eventually decided to release the chaplain and soldiers. The chaplain demanded compensation of $50,000 (later reduced to $25,000) for his lost property, or he would burn the town. The people refused, and the angry chaplain finally left empty-handed. Word spread of the threat to burn the town, and more than a dozen of the liberated blacks came back and, amazingly, offered to surrender themselves to the Confederates to spare the town from the flames. Fortunately for all, the chaplain did not return.[21]

At least one black hostage freed himself: "One negro effected his escape by shooting and seriously wounding his rebel guard. He forced the gun from the rebel and fired, wounding [him?] in the head, and then skedaddled." Others were not as fortunate in their resistance. A Vermont soldier wrote to his wife on July 15 that he had found a black male, barely alive, left in a barn by "the Rebels." His body had been mutilated and burned apparently "because he would not go over the river with them."[22]

No one knows how many African Americans were seized in Pennsylvania. The fates of many are also unknown. The *Mercerburg Journal* stated that "some of these unfortunates were brought back, or found their way home again after six months or a year. Others were never returned or heard of afterward." The fact that blacks were taken prisoner is corroborated by Confederate prison records and by records of the Freedmen's Bureau. Amos Bares, a free black from Pennsylvania, was freed from a Richmond prison by order of the War Department. A Richmond minister petitioned for his release in apparent response to a request from a Pennsylvania Presbyterian minister. Some blacks from Pennsylvania may have been sent to Southern prisons instead of slavery because of sabotage or other interference with the Confederate army as they passed through the state.[23]

Reverend Scaff indicated that irregulars did the kidnapping of blacks and that the regular army was better behaved. The Southern soldier who refused Jemima Cree's request to free her friend Mag justified his actions by saying that he was following orders. The Franklin Repository indicates, "Quite a number of Negroes were stolen by the army of Gen. Lee, and evidently with the sanction of officers." No evidence shows exactly where such orders might have originated and how high on the chain of command went knowledge of these practices. On July 1, however, Lieutenant General James Longstreet, Commander of the First Corps of the Army of Northern Virginia, instructed one of his division commanders, George E. Pickett, "the commanding general [Lee] desires you to come on this evening as far as this point." In the *same paragraph* he instructs Pickett, "The captured contraband had better be brought along with you for further disposition." Longstreet ranked as senior corps commander—therefore, second in command to Lee. It is certainly possible that Lee knew nothing about this practice but not likely. Lee was usually well aware of what his army was doing and surely should have been familiar with the orders emanating from his second in command.[24]

Black Volunteers in the Gettysburg Campaign

Even people very knowledgeable about the Civil War hold the mistaken notion that no blacks fought against the invading Confederates or that no black soldiers were killed in the Gettysburg Campaign. Although many blacks fled or hid from the invaders, many stepped forward to fight. Long before the June invasion had begun, African Americans in this part of Pennsylvania added their names to the fight. To the west of Gettysburg lies the town of Chambersburg in Franklin County, Pennsylvania. This town was already known as a center for the fight for freedom. Here the white abolitionist John Brown planned and recruited volunteers for his plan to free slaves in Virginia. At a quarry outside of Chambersburg, Brown met with black abolitionist Frederick Douglass seeking support for his raid on Harpers Ferry. Douglass, doubtful that the plan would work, declined the invitation to join, but a younger black man accompanying Douglass, Shields Green, decided to "go with the old man."

The government officials of Pennsylvania hesitated to raise black troops, even after Lincoln's authorization in January 1863, but Massachusetts governor John Andrew quickly sent out a call for black soldiers to fill the ranks of the Fifty-fourth and Fifty-fifth Massachusetts Regiments. Black citizens of Franklin County responded with enthusiasm. The *Valley Spirit* in its April 29, 1863, issue announced the departure of "some forty or fifty black recruits for the Massachusetts Regiments." By the time the great Rebel invasion had begun, these men already wore the uniform of the U.S. Army. When they heard of the invasion, they ached to be part of the force that drove back the Southern tide. But in June 1863 they occupied part of South Carolina's seacoast, a thousand miles away, preparing to take on the rebellion on its home ground. In their letters home, they expressed the frustration of being beyond where they could protect their own families. Early in the Gettysburg Campaign, Chambersburg fell to the advancing Confederates.

Black Franklin County residents serving in the South wrote home, "i Wod like to now how you got a long this sommer i had heard that the rebel Was in that part and I hard that had a hard time With them." Jacob Christy later said, "I am a soldier myself and I know what fighting is the compy that I belong to has 80 some men in it and I know that we can wipe the best 200 rebels that they can fetch to us . . . let us get where thay are."

In Gettysburg, black citizens also stepped forward as volunteers. At least three weeks before the great battle, a "Colored Company" had already been formed. Gettysburg resident Henry J. Fannestock wrote on June 10, 1863, "The Colored Company here under command of Capt Randolph Johnston have offered their services to Gov Andrew of Mass. But have understood since that they will not be allowed to leave the state, but will join a Colored Regt. or Brigade to be formed in this state."[25]

This letter is one of the few written references to a company of African American volunteers raised in Gettysburg. David Wills, one of the town's leading citizens, sent a telegram to Governor Andrew G. Curtin offering these troops to help stop the enemy advance. Apparently in haste, Wills wrote,

Gettysburg June 15

Honorable A G Curtin

There can be a company of sixty colored volunteers obtained here—Will they be accepted

David Wills

Curtin responded,

David Wills,

We have no authority to accept colored men in this new service. Authority must first be obtained from the War Dept.

A. G. Curtin[26]

Lee's incursion into Pennsylvania did wonders for overcoming that state's opposition to raising black troops. Governor Andrew G. Curtin's initial call for volunteers to defend the state did not specify race. Reports of the invasion reached Philadelphia by the fifteenth of June. That city's mayor, Alexander Henry, echoed the governor's call, and Philadelphia's black community responded. Amid the sound of emotional speeches and the call of fife and drum, packed black churches held spirited meetings to discuss their response. Posters cried out:

MEN OF COLOR

Of Philadelphia!
The Country Demands your Services. The Enemy is Approaching. You Know his object. It is to Subjugate the North and Enslave us. Already many of our Class in this State have been Captured and Carried South to Slavery, Stripes and Mutilation. For our own sake and for the sake of our Common Country we are called upon now to
Come Forward!
Let us seize this great opportunity of vindicating our manhood and patriotism through all time. The General Commanding at this post is arranging for the
Defense of the City!
He will need the aid of every Man who can shoulder a musket or handle a pick. We have assured him of the readiness of our people to do their whole duty in the emergency. We need not ask you to justify us in having made this assurance. The undersigned have been designated a Committee to have the matter in charge. Members of this Committee will sit every day at
BETHEL CHURCH, cor. of 6th & Lombard Streets
And At
Union Church, Coates Street below York Avenue
Their business will be to receive the Names of all Able Bodied Men of Color who are willing to share with others the burdens and duties of Entrenching and Defending the City. Men of Color! you who are able and willing to fight or labor in the work now to be done, call immediately and report yourselves at one or the other of the above places[27]

One black Philadelphia institution that was sure to respond enthusiastically to the call for volunteers was the Institute for Colored Youth. The dynamic young leader Octavius Catto taught here and inspired many students to step forward with him. All of the teachers at the institute were black. The school specialized in producing teachers, including the first to be accepted into the faculty of Philadelphia public schools. The school's principal, Ebenezer D. Bassett, was wary about how the black volunteers, including his teachers and students, would be treated. Would they be treated on an equal basis with white troops? On June 16, Bassett sent a letter to Mayor Henry expressing his hesitation to participation without the answers to several questions. He asked if the volunteers would be released from their obligation after the invaders were repelled or would they be held beyond that time. He also asked if they would be under state or Federal authority and if they would be issued arms before leaving the city. Finally, if they became casualties, would their families be entitled to the same consideration as the families of white casualties? The mayor responded that it was his understanding that the men would serve only for the present emergency, that they would be under Federal authority, and that "arms and necessary accouterments will be furnished." On the final concern, Henry could only say, "The mayor can give no guarantee in case of death or wound, as to extending aid to the family of those killed or disabled, but has no doubt that they will receive the same consideration as other troops."

Philadelphia's black volunteers numbered ninety and quickly filled an entire company. The City Arsenal at Broad and Race Streets issued the men clothing and equipment, but they would have to wait for their arrival in Harrisburg to get rifles. They speedily headed to the train station for a tearful but proud departure for Harrisburg. Parents of some of the young volunteers thought that they were too young to be going off to war and stepped in to spirit them away. One student from the institute, Joseph G. Anderson Jr., was seized at the station by his parents but escaped and reunited with his comrades. One student called this day "the most exciting I ever witness, we went to see the boys start for harrisburg." Philadelphia had raised its first unit of black soldiers.[28]

The train left for Harrisburg only two days after Governor Curtin had rejected the black volunteers from Gettysburg. The governor was apparently unaware of the developments in Philadelphia. Federal officers in Harrisburg probably voiced to Curtin their objection to raising black troops, even for this emergency. The governor fired off a blunt telegram to Mayor Henry, "Have the negroes stopped at once." The train had already left Philadelphia, but complying with the governor's wishes, Henry attempted to intercept the Harrisburg-bound train at the intervening West Chester station with the telegraphed instructions, "Stop Negroe volunteers now at West Chester from leaving." Henry also was too late.

The volunteers reached Harrisburg eager to fight. The commander of that department, Major General Darius N. Couch, however, dashed the hopes of the black volunteers. Declaring that he was authorized to accept only sixty-day volunteers, he rejected outright these thirty-day volunteers. When Mayor Henry heard of Couch's decision, he became an advocate for the black volunteers, asking, "Is there not some mistake? I urge their acceptance by you as highly expedient in every view." Curtin, however, informed Henry that he had already sent them back to Philadelphia. The dejected recruits returned to Philadelphia, disappointed and frustrated but determined. In hindsight, this bureaucratic decision, made at the height of the need for volunteers, seems inconceivable. The rejected men believed that race had to be a factor in this decision. Washington agreed, and Secretary of War Edwin M. Stanton shortly afterward sent a telegram to Couch instructing him to accept volunteers "regardless of race." That telegram came too late for that first company to participate in the Gettysburg Campaign, but those rejected soldiers soon formed the core of Company A of the Third Regiment of U.S. Colored Infantry, the first regiment of black troops raised in Pennsylvania.

Family and sweethearts of the young volunteers may have secretly sighed in relief at the rejection. Emilie Davis confided to her diary, "This morning the first thing that I heard was that the boys had been sent back. I feel glad and sorry," and "We all are so thankful that our boys are all home again." But she observed, "The boys are still talking about going to war."

The War Department sent to Philadelphia George Stearns, who had been one of the "Secret Six" who gave financial support to John Brown's activities. Stearns took charge of raising and organizing of black troops in the city. He quickly contacted Stanton that two companies were ready to deal with the emergency, but Stanton hesitated to use them against the invading army in Pennsylvania because of the opposition in Harrisburg. He telegraphed Stearns:

> This morning I saw the dispatch referred to in your telegram, and immediately telegraphed General Couch that he was authorized to receive troops without regard to color; but if there is likely to be any dispute about the matter, it would be better to send no more. It is well to avoid all controversy in the present juncture, as the troops can be well used elsewhere.[29]

Defending Harrisburg

In late June, the Southern army threatened to cross the Susquehanna River and capture Harrisburg. Sunday, June 28, Robert E. Lee sent orders to his corps commanders, instructing Lieutenant General Richard Ewell to take Harrisburg with Lieutenant General James Longstreet in support. Capturing Harrisburg would enable the Rebels to cut the Pennsylvania Railroad between the state capital and Philadelphia and to gather massive supplies, but first they would have to overcome their only significant obstacle, the Susquehanna River. State and local officials urged volunteers to help fortify the city. Fortunately, just at the time that heavy labor was needed for the defense of the capital, hundreds of refugees fleeing the advancing army surged toward the city. Many of these refugees came from the Gettysburg area, including some of the black residents. Many black laborers went to work shoring up the city's defenses. General Couch had to acknowledge their contributions:

> The heights on the right bank of the Susquehanna, opposite to Harrisburg, were being fortified, in order to cover that city and the important bridges.

Some of the patriotic citizens of that city volunteered to work in the trenches; others were paid. The colored population were not behind their white brethren in giving assistance.[30]

Harrisburg, as most Northern towns, struggled with race relations. A number of racial riots had occurred over the years that had inflicted personal injury and property destruction on the black community. The idea of armed black volunteers was so unthinkable for so many whites that any black citizen desiring to volunteer would have to go elsewhere to offer his services to the military. On March 9, 1863, fourteen black men from towns west of Harrisburg, some in uniform, passed through the city by train on their way to Massachusetts where that state had begun organizing the Fifty-fourth Massachusetts Regiment.

As Pennsylvania continued to reject black volunteers, Harrisburg's men of color decided to volunteer their services where they would be appreciated. A local black journalist and community leader, Thomas Morris Chester, helped organize recruits for Massachusetts regiments. Thirty recruits left by railroad over the June 6–7 weekend, and 130 more volunteers from Harrisburg and adjoining Cumberland County left two days later.

Some Pennsylvanians became disturbed about the increasing number of black residents quitting the state for the welcoming arms of the Bay State. The *Philadelphia Inquirer* reported that "Pennsylvania has already lost fully 1500 men who have enlisted in Massachusetts." Self-interest fueled much of this concern. As the stream of white volunteers continued to dry up, the Federal government set a quota of soldiers to be provided by each state. Should the state fail to meet the quota, it would have to draft to fill the shortfall. The *Daily Telegraph* complained,

How Many Colored Troops Has Pennsylvania Furnished?
   This question is asked daily, and we have taken the pains to ascertain the number, as near as possible. Last evening we were reliably informed that the squad of one hundred and thirty-five negro recruits, then leaving, would make a total of one thousand one hundred and fifty five men. Pennsylvania, in all probability, is not credited for a single man of these recruits, and, when the draft comes, we will have to furnish just as many men as though these colored recruits had never left the State.[31]

The very morning that the 130 black volunteers departed from Harrisburg, Union and Confederate cavalry clashed in the Battle of Brandy Station, a preliminary to the great Confederate offensive. A captured slave of a Southern officer revealed that Pennsylvania was about to be invaded.

Harrisburg stood out as a tempting prize. Attractive targets there included railroad and canal connections, key bridges and turnpikes, and a rich store of supplies. Adding to the attraction of the city were Camp Curtin, the largest Union training camp, and the morale boost from capturing the capital city of such a significant Northern state. Governor Andrew G. Curtin issued a plea specifically to the black community to step forward as defenders. The Governor also ordered a halt to black Pennsylvanians leaving the state to enlist elsewhere:

Whereas, Information has been received from the War Department, "that the State will receive credit for all enlistments of colored men who may be mustered into the United States service as Pennsylvania troops, *under the authority of the War Department*, and that no credit can be allowed for individuals who leave the State and are mustered into organizations elsewhere;"

It is ordered—

I. All persons are prohibited from raising colored volunteers in Pennsylvania otherwise than under the authority of the War Department, to recruit in Pennsylvania.

II. The people of color in Pennsylvania are forbidden to enlist in or attach themselves to any organization of colored volunteers to be furnished from other States.

III. All magistrates, district attorneys and officers of the Commonwealth, are required to arrest and prosecute all persons who shall disobey this general order, and particularly all persons, their aiders and abettors, who, under any pretended authority shall enlist colored volunteers for any brigade, regiment, battery or company, to be furnished from other States, or who shall advertise and open or keep recruiting stations for such enlistments, excepting under the authority of the War Department to recruit in Pennsylvania, so that such offenders may be brought to justice.[32]

The city needed muscle power to quickly build substantial fortifications to hold off the invaders. The *Harrisburg Patriot and Union* contained an advertisement for laborers:

TO THE COLORED MEN OF HARRISBURG

We want men of muscle, and men who are ready and willing to work on our entrenchments.—We have such white men already. But colored men can help in this common cause also, and colored men are needed at this crisis.—Liberal inducements are offered to such of those as assist us, and their pay will [be] $1.25 per day as long as they work. The night laborers will receive the same compensation.—Turn out then men of all classes and colors, if for nothing

Pennsylvania citizens digging fortifications to protect Harrisburg from the invading Rebels. Hundreds of African Americans took part in this labor. This engraving by F. H. Bellew first appeared in the New York Illustrated News.

more, to the assistance of your country, and the capital of the old Keystone State.

Hundreds of black refugees fleeing northward poured into the capital city, where Harrisburg's African American community provided them with food, shelter, and a chance to wash off the dust of their flight. Beyond this hospitality, however, the new arrivals might still observe signs that they were less than welcome. Missing or cracked window panes on black homes still bore witness to the recent two nights of antiblack race riots. Some refugees arrived in Harrisburg in military wagons. They had the good fortune to be picked up in their flight by sympathetic teamsters who were themselves fleeing from the advancing Southern army after General Milroy's defeat at Winchester.

This act of kindness by the teamsters stood out as an aberration from the indifference or callousness displayed by other Pennsylvanians during their flight. The *Patriot and Union* pointed out, "We noticed the train for Carlisle going out as usual yesterday morning. Among those returning was a large number of negroes, who had fled down the valley a day or two before, lest they might fall into the 'hands of the Philistines.'"

In addition to those working on the fortifications themselves, other blacks labored on the several powerful fire engine pumps, forcing water from the Susquehanna through fire hoses up to the fort where it would be stored in barrels for the coming siege. The long handles of the pumps required eight to ten men on each side to generate enough sustained pressure to propel water from the river up the high bluff to Hummel Hill, site of the fortifications built to protect the capital. Newspapers praised these workers: "We are informed by the managers of the Citizens fire company, now in this service of supplying water to Fort Couch, that the contrabands detailed to assist them are faithful and efficient workers."

The supply of black labor continued to swell as new arrivals came to Harrisburg by every available means of transport. Some local news reporters as well as visiting New Yorkers recounted with empathy the plight of the refugees. The *New York Herald* reported,

A train of cars came down this afternoon. It was filled with people escaping from Carlisle. Among the collection was a large number of contrabands. Throughout the entire day wagons of all descriptions loaded with furniture and other property, have been coming into town. It is enough to touch the most obdurate heart to see the poor blacks as then come to this common asylum. Several of them walked the entire distance from Carlisle, and the feet of many were swollen and bleeding.[33]

A reporter from the *Telegraph* also cast a sympathetic eye toward the displaced people and called on the local citizenry to help them in their time of need:

The Harrisburg Bridge—This outlet for thousands of refugees from up the Cumberland Valley was thronged with a moving mass of beings pouring into this city all day, and new arrivals from up the valley surpassed anything we ever saw. Wagon load after wagon load of men, women and children poured into the city from morning till night, many of them contrabands and free negroes, seeking to escape from the grasp of the Southern rebels. The sight of these defenseless people was truly pitiful, but few of them knowing which way to turn, and all depending on the generosity of the people east of the Susquehanna for support and sustenance. Where many of them go, after reaching this city, we know not, but many remain in our midst, unable to sustain themselves without aid from our citizens, numbers of whom have plenty to give, and will give, willingly, without a murmur or feeling of regret.

The newcomers became a source of curiosity for the townspeople. The residents hoped to glean from the refugees some intelligence regarding the approaching invaders.

A Motley Group—A party of thirty negroes from Chambersburg and vicinity came over the bridge this morning, and stopped to refresh themselves in the Front Street Park, a short distance from the bridge. While there they attracted much attention from passers-by, and many inquiries were made concerning the whereabouts of the rebel army, and their probable strength. The poor negroes, as a matter of course, had never seen the rebel army, or they would not have been here, but they answered the questions as near as they could, the questioners going away evidently satisfied with the information received. Like many of the other refugees from up the valley, they had no place to go to, and appeared lost in this section of the country.

Finally, Harrisburg officials authorized the city's African Americans to form a military company. Overcoming considerable white resistance, Harrisburg's first black militia unit formed and drilled under the command of local black citizen Henry Bradley. The city's black population cheered them as they marched through the streets.

As that company drilled, Thomas Morris Chester busily organized a second company, bringing the city's African American volunteers to 120. The black recruits were denied rifles until the sound of Confederate cannon barely two miles away sent shivers through the capital. The black companies, now 150 strong, hastened to the state arsenal on Walnut Street to receive their muskets. They became "the first company of blacks ever armed by the state of Pennsylvania." At sundown, they crossed the bridge and took their position on the fortified heights.[34]

The coming fight would mean casualties. Hospitals would be needed, and buildings would have to be prepared for that service. One of the buildings so prepared was the African American Presbyterian Church at Walnut Street and River Alley. The battle for which they had prepared, however, never happened. Orders from Robert E. Lee directed corps commander Richard Ewell to break off his campaign against Harrisburg and concentrate to the south.

Henry Bradley and T. M. Chester petitioned General Couch for their companies to be mustered officially as state troops and to authorize black officers to command them. By late June, Adjutant General Lorenzo Thomas had arrived in Harrisburg. Speaking for the Federal government, he responded that black volunteers should not be entered into state service but should be sent to Camp William Penn, near Philadelphia, where they were to be mustered into Federal service within the newly created Bureau of United States Colored Troops.

The welcome quickly wore out for black refugees in the city once the threat of Confederate attack had passed. With the invader gone, white citizens wanted the "Contraband" gone as well. Police gathered up any people of color who were not known to be permanent Harrisburg residents.

> Over three hundred negroes, of both sexes, were collected near the Mayor's office yesterday afternoon by the policemen. They were all fugitives from up the Cumberland Valley, and had been collected together in order that the Mayor might have transportation furnished them to their various homes. They presented a most singular appearance;—some of them as jolly as their nature would allow, while others looked as though they lost every friend they ever had on earth. Many of the males had been employed on the entrenchments, but these are about finished, and no work that they could do, which would be of any interest to the Government remained undone. They were sent up the valley last evening in an extra train.

Even after the expulsion, the remaining refugees, many of whom had found jobs and become new members of the community, were subject to harassment and assault. One young man who had become a servant to a Union officer became the victim of an unprovoked, senseless, and nearly fatal shooting by a white soldier. Another black man refused to comply when asked by soldiers to unload a train car for them; he was bayoneted.[35]

The threat of invasion had made African Americans tolerable in Harrisburg. When the danger vanished, tolerance disappeared with it.

The Battle of Wrightsville

Another key bridge spanned the Susquehanna southeast of Harrisburg, connecting the towns of Columbia and Wrightsville. The Columbia-Wrightsville Bridge, then considered the largest covered bridge in the world, measured a mile and a quarter in length. It was unusually wide for that type of span because it accommodated both railroad and wagon traffic side by side. Confederate seizure of this bridge would all but ensure the capture of Harrisburg.

Steven Smith, "one of the wealthiest black men in the country," made major investments in the Columbia Bridge Company and in the bank that financed its construction. He had made his fortune in lumber and real estate. For many years the Columbia-Wrightsville Bridge served as a significant conduit for escaped slaves. "Columbus' free black merchants regularly welcomed the runaways and helped them on a journey that often ended in Canada." Much of this aid was backed financially by Steven Smith and William Whipper.

This area witnessed dramatic games of deception played by both sides. Spies in league with slave catchers kept the bridge under constant surveillance. Freight cars crossing the bridge sometimes carried hidden escapees from slavery. During the transition across the bridge, the cars would detach from the locomotive and be hitched to mules and horses for the crossing. This was an especially tense time for the clandestine passengers, since the cars were sometimes searched before crossing. The enclosed bridge served to magnify sounds during the slow mile across the river. Wagons also surreptitiously carried similar cargo. These wagons were often stopped and searched. "Consignments for 'respectable' businesses in Columbia and Marietta sometimes contained families or individuals illegally smuggled into Lancaster County."

People of color made up a significant portion of the local population. In 1860, Wrightsville's 1,294 townspeople included 169 blacks; in Columbia, it was 437 out of about 5,500. Many had direct connection with the great bridge. Some had helped to build it; others labored on the railroads and canals that used it. Many also worked at the Maultsby-Case Rolling Mill and at local iron furnaces, working side by side with whites.

When Confederates invaded Pennsylvania in June 1863, refugees swelled the traffic over the bridge. A local resident observed blacks mostly on foot carrying huge loads, including parts of beds. Others could not carry many household goods because they carried their children. Columbia resident Sidney Josephine Myer entered in her diary that "immense numbers of refugees came into our town" from York County, but as they entered, many of Columbia's black residents fled. Myer relates that "hundreds of poor negroes walked from Columbia. The roads are lined with them."[36]

On the way to Wrightsville, the Confederates captured the town of York. Little did the Southerners know that this would be the largest town they would capture during the invasion of Pennsylvania. At the town square in York, two striking multistory buildings "dominated the scene." William C. Goodridge, a black businessman, owned one of them. Although born in slavery in Maryland, he obtained his freedom and moved to Pennsylvania. Local residents believed that he used his York emporium and his house at 123 East Philadelphia Street to shelter slaves refugees in their quest for freedom. Rumors related that for several years Goodridge had secreted fugitives in freight cars and whisked them across the Columbia-Wrightsville Bridge.

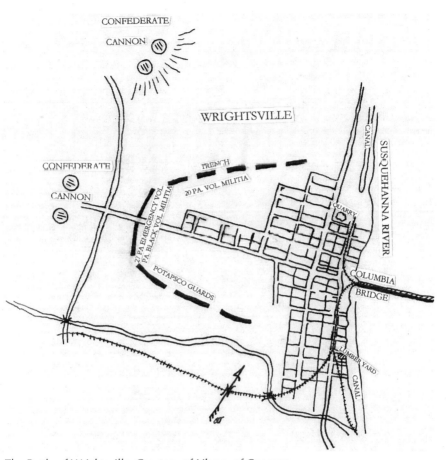

The Battle of Wrightsville. Courtesy of Library of Congress.

About a dozen informal companies from Lancaster County arrived in Wrightsville to offer their assistance in defending the bridge. Many of these companies were sent home at one point, including the black volunteers from Case's Rolling Mill, but about 175 men from Columbia forming four companies returned to Wrightsville, arriving about midnight to reinforce Frick's fragile line of defense. Fifty-three of these men were black.

Answering the call to defend their homeland, black citizens of Columbia and the vicinity formed a company of militia. This all-black unit joined three white companies and, on the night of June 27, marched across the river to Wrightsville. On that side of the river, Colonel Jacob G. Frick commanded a small unit, the Twenty-seventh Pennsylvania Emergency Volunteers. He welcomed the support of the four new companies. Frick made plans to estab-lish a defensive position to repel the Confederates who were heading in their direction by way of York. Some entrenchments had already been constructed by local militia, including dozens of black employees of a nearby rolling mill. The colonel saw that more preparation was needed, and he ordered the men to dig entrenchments on either side of the turnpike. Military and railroad personal had gathered a large supply of tools for digging the necessary en-trenchments.

The soldiers of the three white companies refused to cooperate. Rather than dig the entrenchments, the men of the three white companies simply walked away. Lieutenant Francis B. Wallace wryly commented, "Sunday morning's sun saw us still undisturbed, and witnessed the departure to Co-lumbia of the white companies of citizens to get their breakfasts. They must have become entirely absorbed in that interesting duty, for they forgot to return. The company of colored men remained with us, their palates either being smaller, or their courage greater than that of the good burghers of Columbia." He continued, "No men on that day worked more faithfully or zealously, than the colored company—Their conduct elicited the admiration of all who saw them."

Frick's own troops and the black volunteers laid down their rifles, picked up entrenching tools, and went to work digging the "rifle-pits." Muscles that had toiled daily in the rolling mills now moved earth. The men dug away, determined to construct sturdy earthworks before the enemy force arrived. Eying the stacked arms waiting for the fight to come while building the de-fenses that they hoped might save their lives, they must have pondered the peril that they were about to face. Fighting while wearing no formal uniform, they could not expect to be treated as prisoners of war. The Rebels carried away unoffending black civilians into slavery. They could expect no better if captured while shooting at the Southern soldiers. Indeed, enraged Confeder-ates might exact immediate revenge.

Frick had only eleven hundred men, one uniformed regiment of militia and an assortment of volunteers, to guard a far-flung defensive perimeter. In the upcoming engagement, his men would have single-shot muskets, requir-ing massed formations to concentrate fire power. The defenders by necessity, however, stood about two yards apart, far too spread out for effective con-centration of fire.[37]

They continued digging until about 5:30 PM, when the enemy arrived at their front. Down went the tools, up came the rifles. The black volunteers took their places, side by side with the Twenty-seventh Pennsylvania, on a slight rise holding the center of the line.

By six o'clock, the Rebel force deployed astride the turnpike three quarters of a mile away, directly in front of the rifle pits. The enemy force, twenty-five hundred strong, included veteran infantry and cavalry and, most menacing of all, artillery. The Confederates tested the left of the Union line with a combined force of cavalry and infantry. They moved against the Union skirmishers posted in advance of the main line. The skirmishers traded rifle fire for a short time but eventually fell back to the main line. The rest of the Union line poured out a steady stream of fire and held back their foes.

The Southerners then placed their artillery on high ground opposite the Union right and positioned two more cannon astride the turnpike at the center of the line. The artillery opened fire. Frick reported, "These guns were used most vigorously against those of my command occupying the rifle-pits." The defenders, having no artillery of their own on that side of the river, were helpless to reply to this cannonade. One cannon shot struck a black defender in the trenches and decapitated him. The *Lancaster Weekly Express* reported, "One of the killed was a negro—whose head was taken off by a shell." The *Reading Daily Times* recorded, "Only one man, a negro, was killed, who had his head taken off by a shell in one of the streets of Wrights-ville." Although multiple newspapers reported the man's death, his identity remains unknown. The slain Columbia man was the first Northerner killed since George Sandoe was shot off his horse near McAllister Mill.

Meanwhile, a column of Confederate infantry slipped around toward the Union right, under cover of the artillery barrage and with high ground concealing their movement. They advanced to within a few hundred yards of the river and sent skirmishers ahead through a field of tall grain that hid them from the view of the defenders. The men in the trenches traded shots with the skirmishers as best they could, but they could see them only briefly when they rose out of the grain to fire.

The situation became desperate for the greatly outnumbered defenders, as artillery pounded their position while infantry threatened to reach the river on both flanks. The Rebels threatened not only to take the bridge but also to cut off the defenders' retreat and capture them as well. After an hour and a quarter of fighting, unable to fulfill the first objective of holding back the invaders, Colonel Frick gave orders for his men to withdraw across the bridge and destroy it to prevent the Rebels from crossing.

The *Pottsville Miners' Journal* reported on July 4 that the retreat was carried out "in excellent order by the command, although exposed during the movement to a heavy fire of shell and to a galling one of sharpshooters." A less complimentary Southern account of the engagement boasted that the Rebels "routed them." In the midst of the tense retreat, an elderly black man kept his composure. A participant observed, "One old negro to whom was entrusted the duty of igniting the fuse sat very coolly on the edge of the pier, smoking a cigar."

Many of the retreating defenders panicked and broke ranks, running across the bridge. In spite of their lack of combat experience, the company of black volunteers remained intact and maintained good order throughout the retreat.

The explosives detonated, but the blast failed to bring down that section of the bridge as planned. The defenders implemented a backup plan, pouring large barrels of coal oil and kerosene over kindling and the oak flooring of the bridge and igniting it. In a few minutes, the magnificent bridge was in flames. The Confederates would not cross. They could claim only the empty victory of taking the militia's entrenchments. The Confederates discovered the headless body of the black defender and buried his remains in the trenches.[38]

Most of the black volunteers camped that night on a hill along Third Street, just beyond Columbia. Some of the men marched off to guard a nearby ford in case the enemy should force a crossing there.

Confederate Major General Jubal A. Early lamented the opportunity that the defenders of the bridge had denied him. He well understood the significance of the defenders' actions:

> I regretted very much the failure to secure this bridge, as, finding the defenseless condition of the country . . . I had determined, if I could get possession of the Columbia Bridge, to cross my division over the Susquehanna, and cut the Pennsylvania Central Railroad, march upon Lancaster, lay that town under contribution, and then attack Harrisburg in the rear while it should be attacked in front by the rest of the corps. . . . This project, however, was entirely thwarted by the destruction of the bridge, as the river was otherwise impassable, being very wide and deep at this point.[39]

In his official report, Colonel Frick lauded the men under his command, but he reserved special praise for the black soldiers:

> Before closing this report, justice compels me to make mention of the excellent conduct of the company of Negroes from Columbia. After working industriously in the rifle-pits all day, when the fight commenced they took their guns and stood up to their work bravely. They fell back only when ordered to do so.[40]

By their conduct at Wrightsville, African American defenders had won new respect for themselves and for the thousands of black volunteers to come. The *Examiner and Herald* said, "The only Columbia volunteers in the fight were fifty-three negroes, who after making entrenchments with the soldiers, took muskets and fought bravely." The men could take pride in "bearing themselves like veteran soldiers." Lt. Wallace wrote, "All honor to the colored men of Columbia. They will die in defense of life and liberty, which is more than a majority of the whites here seem disposed to do."

Most of the black volunteers returned to their jobs at Case's Rolling Mill. Some of them joined regiments of the U.S. Colored Troops. One of them was John Aquilla Wilson, who enlisted in the Thirty-second Regiment of United States Colored Infantry and trained at Camp William Penn. Wilson survived to be the last living Civil War veteran in York County and lived to hear of the Japanese attack on Pearl Harbor. He died in 1942 at the age of 101.[40]

On the Gettysburg Battlefield

Cemetery Hill
At the crest of Cemetery Hill stands an equestrian statue of Major General Oliver Otis Howard, commander of XI Corps, which helped defend this hill. Earlier in the war, Howard had lost his right arm at the Battle of Fair Oaks. Near the end of the war, he accepted the position of commissioner of the Bureau of Freedmen, Refugees, and Abandoned Lands, better known as "The Freedmen's Bureau." This organization was established to help newly freed blacks make the transition to freedom. The agency provided clothing and food and supervised labor contracts to prevent exploitation of the former slaves. It also established hospitals and schools.

Howard hired Frederick Douglass's son, Charles, for a bureau position. When the other clerks voiced their objection to hiring a man of color, the general threatened to fire them all and replace them with blacks. Famed abolitionist Sojourner Truth addressed him as "Friend Howard." The general served as commissioner through the entire life of the bureau. In tribute to his work, Howard University, perhaps the finest of the historically black colleges, bears his name.[41]

Culp's Hill
Although many Federal soldiers remained indifferent to slavery, the Union ranks included some ardent abolitionists, such as Thomas L. Kane. Before the war, Kane had written many newspaper articles advocating abolition. He served as U.S. district commissioner at the time Congress passed the Fugitive Slave Law. Enforcing that law would violate his conscience, and so he

submitted his letter of resignation. The district judge, who happened to be his own father, considered Thomas's letter to be in contempt of the law. He had his son thrown in jail. Fortunately, the U.S. Supreme Court intervened on behalf of the younger Kane. Once free, he became an active agent for the Underground Railroad.

Kane volunteered for military service when the war began. By the time of the Gettysburg Campaign, he had risen to command a brigade, but pneumonia had forced him into a hospital. At the news of the Confederate invasion of his native Pennsylvania, he rose from his bed to rejoin his comrades in arms, although he was too weak even to sit on a horse. Kane's brigade defended the slopes of Culp's Hill. Dug in near the cave of the "Black Ducks," the brigade held its ground against repeated attacks.[42]

One of the Confederate brigades that it repelled from Culp's Hill was the famous "Stonewall" Brigade. This unit had once been commanded by Gen. Thomas J. "Stonewall" Jackson. A free black man, Jim Lewis, had served as the general's cook, servant, and confidant. Lewis is a character featured in the book and motion picture *Gods and Generals*. Jackson was killed in the last major battle before Gettysburg, at Chancellorsville. Lewis barely had time to mourn the loss of Jackson before rejoining the Army of Northern Virginia. He accompanied Col. "Sandie" Pendelton, an officer in the "Stonewall Brigade."[43]

In a field just beyond Culp's Hill, the Second Massachusetts Regiment went into battle without one of its young former officers. Captain Robert Gould Shaw had served in that unit through the early part of the war but had left his comrades earlier in 1863 to take command of the soon-to-be legendary Fifty-fourth Massachusetts Regiment. Many of Shaw's former comrades would die here at Gettysburg in a doomed assault against troops behind a stone wall at the foot of Culp's Hill. That same month, Shaw would lead his new black regiment in another futile attack. In that attack—on Fort Wagner, near Charleston, South Carolina—Shaw would fall beside hundreds of his comrades.[44]

Devil's Den and Little Round Top

On the second day of the battle, the First Division of Daniel E. Sickles's III Corps defended the entire Union line from Devil's Den to the Sherfy Peach Orchard. Brigadier General David B. Birney, one of the most passionate opponents of slavery among the Union generals, commanded this division. In spite of minor wounds, he took over the corps when a cannonball took off Sickles's leg. Birney did not survive the war but died October 18, 1864, of disease contracted during his war service. Birney's father, James G. Birney, also an ardent abolitionist, had published an antislavery newspaper and was tried for violation of the Fugitive Slave Act. He had run for president twice as the candidate of the antislavery Liberty Party. He had also inspired his other son, William, with the abolitionist spirit. William recruited thousands of black soldiers and eventually commanded a division of U.S. Colored Troops.

Some of the most vicious fighting at Gettysburg took place in the assault of Major General John B. Hood's division against the Union left flank on the second day of the battle. Fighting raged near a small farmhouse owned by George Weikert about four hundred yards west by northwest of Devil's Den. (Five years after the battle, he would sell the farm to a black man, John Timbers. Timbers would add to the small log house. Written accounts and maps of the Battle of Gettysburg often refer to this dwelling as the "Timbers House," although Timbers himself did not live in the house until after the battle. He did live here, however, in the early 1870s, when Southerners sponsored the work of reclaiming the many Confederate bodies that had been buried on and near his property.) Early in the fighting, the First Texas and the Third Arkansas regiments surged past the house. Later, Henry L. Benning's Georgia Brigade advanced, passing by what would become Timbers's house and through his fields. The stone walls on the property were hotly fought over because they gave valuable cover to either attacker or defender.

Eventually, George "Tige" Anderson's Georgia Brigade advanced in support, stampeding whatever cattle still remained around the farm buildings. Finally, Joseph B. Kershaw's South Carolina and Paul J. Semmes's Georgia brigades of Maj. Gen. Lafayette McLaw's division charged across the field between the John Rose house and the Timbers house, taking heavy casualties. The Southerners eventually captured Devil's Den but paid a considerable price for it; three days later, Confederate dead would still lie in those fields where they had fallen. By that time, the Rebel army had withdrawn, and photographers Alexander Gardner and Timothy O'Sullivan arrived on the scene. Gardner and O'Sullivan proceeded to take photographs of these combatants who were killed in the field between the Timbers and Rose houses. These photographs and those of a soldier in Devil's Den, also about four hundred yards from the Timbers House, remain the best-known images of dead Confederates at Gettysburg.[45]

Authors and battlefield guides have conferred the title of "Savior of Little Round Top" upon a number of people, including Brig. Gen. Gouverneur K. Warren, Col. Joshua Chamberlain, and Col. Strong Vincent (promoted to brigadier general on his deathbed). Vincent was the only one of the three to sacrifice his life defending that key position. A white private, Oliver W. Norton, carried the flag of Vincent's brigade and accompanied the colonel during much of the battle. When Vincent received his mortal wound and the fighting became even more desperate, Norton hid his horse and flag behind the rocks, obtained a musket, and fought side by side with his old regiment, the Eighty-third Pennsylvania.

After the battle, Norton volunteered to take on a position in one of the new black regiments, the Eighth Regiment of United States Colored Infantry. He would again fight beside brave men in battle; this time, they would be black soldiers. Seven of the soldiers in his regiment were African Americans who hailed from Gettysburg. In one battle alone, three of these soldiers would be wounded, one fatally. Norton would write a number of letters of condolence to the families of fallen black heroes. One of these letters would come to Gettysburg.[46]

James Warfield and his family lived near Seminary Ridge, along the Wheatfield Road, just west of Emittsburg Road. Their thirteen acres included a farm, a solid stone home, and a frame blacksmith shop. Warfield enjoyed great success as a blacksmith, operating two hearths. His shop was known as a "fine location for the blacksmith business, being a No. 1 stand, commanding a large and steady run of customers." Neighbors agreed that he ran "one of the best blacksmith stands in the county."

About noon on July 2, 1863, the Union sharpshooters of Colonel Hiram Berdan's brigade marched by the Warfield place on their way to confront the advancing Confederates of Marcellus C. Wilcox's brigade of Lt. Gen. A. P. Hill's Corp. After delaying the gray troops, the Federals pulled back and left that area in the hands of the Rebels. Kershaw's brigade formed near there for an attack, the Eighth South Carolina lining up near the Warfield House. The Confederates then placed artillery to the east of Warfield's home where the guns could pound Sickles's corps at the Peach Orchard and along Emittsburg Road. James Longstreet pitched his tent west of the Warfield home and may have used the house for a time as his headquarters.

The home was never used as a hospital, but some wounded Confederates were brought there. It may have missed the fate of being formally designated as a field hospital either because it was Longstreet's headquarters or because it stood too close to the action. But Warfield was doomed to suffer considerable loss. Blacksmith equipment such as anvils and bellows was high on the Confederate list of desired items for "acquisition" during the incursion into Pennsylvania. The Southern Army walked away with everything of any value in Warfield's home, barn, or shop. He lost two head of cattle, three hogs, and $516 worth of wheat and corn. All of his buildings, as well as his orchard and gardens, suffered serious injury. Warfield was never compensated for his loss. A year after the battle, he put his property up for sale but had no takers. He moved to Cashtown in 1871 and died four years later.[47]

Across the no-man's land from Confederate-occupied Seminary Ridge ran a nearly parallel rise called Cemetery Ridge. Along this ridge sat two African American farms, those of Abraham Brien and John Fisher. Abraham Brien (spelled "Bryan" in postwar accounts), a descendant of Sydney O'Brien, owned a farm just south of town. He had been born in Maryland, but his children were born in Pennsylvania. Brien's children attended the Granite Schoolhouse with other children of the township. Twice widowed, he lived with his third wife, Elizabeth. Several buildings stood on his twenty-acre property, including a barn, a wagon shed, a corncrib, and a small wood-frame weatherboard home. Brien also rented out at least one small one-story shack along the Emmitsburg Road. The 1860 census shows that he rented one to Mag Palm.

Brien prospered, successfully raising several crops, including wheat, hay, and barley on his twelve acres. He also maintained a small orchard near his house. While developing his farm and clearing the land for tilling, he stacked up rocks and built a stone wall that extended down the ridge. His farm sat on the soon-to-be-famous battle site, Cemetery Ridge, near the epicenter of the climactic fighting that would spell victory or defeat on a hot July day in 1863. Behind Brien's farmhouse, the land sloped upward to the hill on which Abraham Lincoln would give his most famous speech. By the time of the Battle of Gettysburg, Bryan was sixty-one years old and had five children by three wives.[48]

On the afternoon of July 3, 1863, Union troops tenaciously fought to defend Cemetery Ridge. Fighting concentrated around the stone wall that separated Brien's exposed barn from the farmhouse behind Union lines. The fight raged to the bitter end around the barn. As one participant described it, "some of Lane's Brigade were stopped within a few feet of the stone wall, fell back and took refuge in the Bryan Barn. They continued to fight until nearly all were killed or captured by the 111th NY which finally surrounded them."

When the shooting subsided, only a scene of destruction remained. "There were scores of dead by the small house where the left of the rebel line advanced, lying just as they were smitten down, as if a thunderbolt had fallen upon the once living mass." The Brien farmhouse was not used as a hospital. This may have been so because the house was too small or because it was already being used as headquarters for Brigadier General Alexander Hays, a division commander in Winfield Scott Hancock's II Corps.[49]

Brien's property was devastated. Five acres of wheat and barley were gone along with his livestock. His house was "riddled and almost destroyed by artillery fire." Union soldiers had pulled out the fences and stripped the siding from the house to fortify their meager breastworks or to fuel campfires. The shack rented to Mag Palm had stood directly in the path of Pickett's Charge. It was completely destroyed, and Brien never rebuilt it.[50]

Black servants attended to many Union officers. Brigadier General John Buford, a division commander in the Cavalry Corps, relied often on his servant Edward. Buford hailed from Kentucky, a slave state, and had a half brother who fought in the Confederate army. Edward, however, was a free man, and he did far more than just hold the general's horse. Buford entrusted Edward with messages for his subordinates. Neither man suffered injury at Gettysburg, but the demands of the service took its toll on the general; before the year was out, he died of illness contracted in the line of duty. A bereaved Edward was at his bedside as he passed away.[51]

The commander of the army of the Potomac, Maj. Gen. George Gordon Meade, hired black attendants throughout the war. According to a long-standing oral tradition, one of the first cannon shots struck in the Leister's yard and killed Meade's black servant. He has been referred to as the first to die in Pickett's Charge. The servant in this story is never named.

Meade's best-known personal servant was a black man named John Marley. Marley accompanied the general through most of the war. Meade paid him a salary for which the army partially reimbursed him. Meade often mentioned Marley in letters to his wife. More than a servant, he was a devoted friend and confidant. Marley stood by the general's side at the Battle of Antietam, but no documentation places him on the Gettysburg battlefield. In Meade's haste to reach the battlefield, he deliberately left behind much of his personal baggage. Marley may have remained behind in Maryland to guard the general's possessions. No evidence indicates that he was injured in this campaign.[52]

The inaccurate account of Marley's wounding may be based either on the death of the black volunteer at the Battle of Wrightsville a few days before or on another incident reported in the unit history of Battery B, First New Jersey Artillery. This account describes a field hospital near the John Patterson House on Cemetery Ridge:

The wounded were removed to Rock Creek. The surgeons had packed up, and the last ambulance containing their instruments was leaving, when about 1 o'clock a shell from one of the two signal guns exploded in the barn. It took the arm off a little negro boy, about 14 years old, a servant of an officer in a New York regiment. We were mounted ready to move out. Capt. Clark sent Alley

Steventon to recall the surgeons. The arm of the boy was amputated. He was placed in the ambulance, and we moved out under fire.

This account gives no indication of the fate of the unfortunate young man. It illustrates the difficulty in assessing black casualties in the Gettysburg Campaign. Servants and auxiliary workers suffering wounds would not be noted. Even the Ordnance Department has maintained no record of casualties among its teamsters.

The Ammunition Train

As the Battle of Gettysburg began to take shape, General Meade realized that he needed to rush as many troops as possible as soon as possible to that crossroads town. He could not afford to clog the roads with wagons; the roads would have to stay clear for the foot soldiers. He ordered the wagon trains to Westminster and Union Bridge in Maryland; the Army of the Potomac arrived at Gettysburg without its supply wagons. One crucial exception to the absence of Union wagons came early in the second day of the battle. About 10:30 on the morning of July 2, Major Freeman McGilvery reported to Brig. Gen. Robert O. Tyler, commander of the artillery reserve. McGilvery had left Taneytown at the break of dawn with the last of the artillery reserve. He also brought the much-needed ammunition train, consisting of seventy wagons. He parked the wagons behind the position of Sickles's III Corps along the Baltimore Pike where it joined the Granite School Road on the west and a dirt road leading to the McAllister Mill on the east side.

McGilvery and others in the artillery reserve engaged in heavy fighting through the afternoon. When night fell, the men unloaded and distributed the needed ammunition. General Tyler reported, "Lieutenant Gillett, First Connecticut Artillery, ordnance officer of this command, was engaged the entire night in issuing ammunition to the batteries of the several corps, as well as those of the Artillery Reserve. Seventy wagons were unloaded, which were sent to the rear on the morning of 3d." Early the next morning, the struggle for Culp's Hill began.

At daylight on July 3, Captain Rigby's battery (A, First Maryland Artillery) opened fire, by direction of Major-general Slocum, upon the troops across Rock Creek moving on our right. The ammunition train and some of the reserve batteries, which had been refitted during the night, were moved up near the Taneytown road.

As Tyler later reported, hostile fire struck the ammunition train:

> Everything was moderately quiet until about 12 o'clock, when, as I was re-
> turning with Captain Robertson from reconnoitering a position for artillery
> opposite our left, the enemy opened a terrific fire of artillery, which, passing
> over the crest of the hill, concentrated behind the lines where the reserve was
> lying. Several officers and men were wounded and animals killed both in the
> batteries and the ammunition train.

Tyler credits the artillery reserve and their ammunition train with making
a major contribution to the repulse of "Pickett's Charge," the deciding action
on the final day of the battle. He concluded,

> I believe it almost unnecessary to speak of the value of the services rendered by
> the Artillery Reserve during the last two days of this action and the great share
> it had in the glorious result. The one hundred and eight guns which were on
> the field were all in position, their fire being concentrated and felt wherever the
> battle was hottest. The skill and gallantry with which they were handled is amply
> attested by the dead of the enemy, slain by shell and canister, lying in their front,
> and the fierce fire under which they did their work is proved by the heavy loss of
> horses and the long record of men and officers killed and wounded.
>   From the ammunition train, as already stated, seventy wagon-loads were is-
> sued on the night of the 2nd to the batteries of the army, and, as shown by the
> report of my ordnance officer, 10,090 rounds were issued to batteries outside of
> the reserve during the battle. The necessity and usefulness of the organization,
> I believe, is beyond a question.

John Fisher, a black farmer, lived on Cemetery Ridge about a half-mile south
of the Bryan house. His farm bristled with activity on the second and third days
of the battle. On July 2, the First Minnesota Regiment rushed forward from its
position southwest of the Fisher farm buildings and hurled itself into the advancing Rebels, who were led by Marcellus C. Wilcox. The regiment stopped
the advance but suffered 82 percent casualties by those engaged this day and
the next. Brig. Gen. John Gibbons's division, temporarily commanded by Brig.
Gen. William Harrow, stood massed north and west of the Fisher farm buildings. Confederate Brig. Gen. A. R. Wright's brigade charged the Union position
on Cemetery Ridge late that afternoon and threatened to break the line. Infantry and artillery units from Fisher Farm met and repulsed the attacking force.[53]

Retreat and Pursuit

By July 4, the outcome of the Battle of Gettysburg had been decided, but the
outcome of the campaign had yet to be determined. Lee could still achieve

success by returning to Virginia with an intact army and also the incredible abundance of supplies it now had.

Confederates had been foraging throughout the campaign. The total amount hauled in would be impossible to determine. The quartermaster of Edward A. O'Nael's brigade, Robert E. Rodes division of Ewell's corps, recorded that in the course of the campaign his brigade had acquired 219 horses and mules, 49,000 pounds of hay, and 46,000 pounds of corn. All of this was taken by but one brigade of the army's thirty-seven brigades of infantry alone. By one historian's calculation, the Army of Northern Virginia captured in Pennsylvania a total of 45,000 head of cattle, 40,000 head of sheep, 25,000 horses and mules, and thousands of hogs. This haul would supply all the military's commissary needs until well after Southern farmers could gather in their fall harvests. But safely bringing home these supplies, along with the miles of ambulances carrying Confederate wounded, would depend on the sweat and skill of his black teamsters.[54]

On the other side, General Meade had won a major victory, but the war would continue as long as the Confederacy kept an army in the field. If the Rebel army could manage to withdraw to Virginia without further damage, the war would go on indefinitely. But if Meade could cut off Lee's line of retreat or pursue aggressively and bring on a decisive battle on this side of the swollen Potomac River, great things could happen. To destroy or capture this army would eliminate the largest Southern army and probably result in the fall of the Confederate capital. The rebellion could be crushed.

On July 5, General Meade informed his corps commanders of his intention to change the army's base of supply from Westminster to Frederick. This move would position the Federal army to strike at the Potomac crossings of Williamsport and Falling Waters before the Confederates could arrive there in force. If Meade had followed through with this order, the six thousand wagons in the Westminster area would have been perfectly situated to support an attack at those crossing points.

But Robert E. Lee did an exceptional job of hiding his movements and concealing his own intent. Meade began to fear that his adversary might be establishing a defensive line in the Pennsylvania mountains and fortifying it into an unassailable position. If that happened, Meade would need to have his supply wagons near at hand. He canceled his orders and held the wagons at Westminster and Union Bridge. If the Union army were forced into attacking Confederates in the mountains, the wagons would need to roll north to Gettysburg to supply it.

Meade had to be concerned not only with the future but also with the immediate needs of his army. Neither the men nor the animals of his army had been regularly fed for days; they had been separated from the quartermaster and commissary wagons. Each of the seven corps commanders would have to reunite his unit with its supply train soon, or pursuit would not begin quickly enough to overtake the withdrawing Confederates.

The success of the Union pursuit would depend on the cavalry. Only that branch could move fast enough to harass or get ahead of the Confederates on their line of retreat. But many horses needed shoeing before they could go anywhere, and all of them needed fodder. Reports finally came to Meade that the Confederate army was not fortifying the mountains but was in full retreat. On the afternoon of July 6, Meade reinstated his orders for a change of base, but by that time thirty precious hours had passed.

The Union cavalry pursued and struck at the Confederates in several small encounters. Brig. Gen. Judson Kilpatrick's division struck the wagon train at Monterey Pass at midnight on July 4–5 amid thunder and lightning. It captured 250 wagons and 1,200 prisoners, including many black teamsters, some of whom would escape and rejoin the Rebel army in Williamsport. Kilpatrick's black servant enthusiastically participated in the destruction of the wagons. Union forces under Robert Milroy also captured black teamsters in an encounter at Cunningham's Crossroads.

At times, the black teamsters in the Confederate wagon train were given arms to defend the wagons. Armed or not, the teamsters were caught in the crossfire and subjected to great danger. As the wagons neared Williamsport, federal cavalry attacked, swooped down on the train, and set fire to the wagons. The flaming wagons, pulled by terrified, sometimes burning horses, bolted through the fields, the teamsters, black laborers, and servants leaping from the burning vehicles. Shells burst among the wagons. Desperately seeking cover, the teamsters and other noncombatants ran into the nearby river, staying as deep as possible. One witness reported seeing "hundreds of black heads just showing above the water. The negro teamsters with one accord had plunged into the river to escape the shells and were submerged to the neck!" Many blacks were captured along with their masters. Guilford, who had appropriated a buggy to evacuate Lt. Col. Green, found himself facing some twenty Federal cavalrymen with pistols aimed at them. He spoke up, "Don't shoot gentlemen, for God's sake don't shoot. We surrender. We are prisoners."

Certainly, many of the black drivers were not volunteers and held no devotion for the Southern cause. After pursuing cavalry overtook a Confederate wagon train, a Union officer saw a driverless wagon filled with Southern prisoners. He asked a nearby black man, perhaps a teamster, perhaps a prisoner of the invaders, "Can you drive that team?" With an affirmative answer, he hopped on the buckboard and, putting his head inside the wagon cover, shouted back to his passengers, "By golly, you toted me off, now I tote you off." Then, "jumping from the box to the back of the saddle mule, with a loud laugh and a yell at the team, he soon had the road clear."

Federal cavalry achieved only limited success in the pursuit because the horses could not carry on without being fed and properly shod. Wesley Merritt's Brigade, for example, lost more than two hundred horses because of inability to feed or shoe them.

Meanwhile, the Army of Northern Virginia set out on an epic journey southward. Success or failure would rest to a great extent on the performance of the army's black teamsters. One historian asserts that over ten thousand black teamsters drove the wagons of the army. He concludes that another ten thousand African Americans accompanied the army as laborers, servants, and cooks. This number agrees with those suggested by contemporary observers, such as Col. James A. Fremantle, as well as other recent historians. The great majority of these teamsters were slaves. Early in the war, the Confederate government had begun leasing slaves from willing owners for twenty dollars per month. After March 1863, the government simply impressed slaves whether the owners agreed or not. Many of the teamsters, however, were free blacks. They were often artisans, blacksmiths, or skilled workers of other types, and they were paid twenty dollars per month. They were called "volunteers," but in an army where even the white soldiers found their terms of enlistment involuntarily extended to the duration of the war, the term appears relative.

A daunting task loomed before them. The wagons of the quartermaster, commissary, and ordnance departments along with the ambulances full of wounded formed a train about fifty-five miles long. Even at a steady speed, this wagon train required over two days to pass any given point.

The road back to Virginia presented a challenge under the best of conditions; weather and war turned it into a nightmare. On July 4 the rains came. By the end of the day, the downpour drenched everyone, including those riding buckboards. The driving rain turned the dirt roads into ribbons of sucking mud. The muck reached sometimes halfway to the hubs. These dirt roads represented the shortest route to the Potomac crossings, but the mud had become such a hindrance that Lee considered countermanding his order and rerouting the wagons onto a more roundabout macadamized road.

The teamsters measured up to the task, driving the teams through the mountain passes and along the torturous narrow roads skirting the mountainsides. They kept on through the night, their way illuminated only by the lightning bolts. Now and then, tragedy struck as a wagon veered off the road and tumbled down the mountainside.

The train eventually reached macadamized roads and converged on Williamsport and Falling Waters, the two planned Potomac crossings. Union cavalry attacked the wagons at Williamsport. The Confederates, including black teamsters who had been handed rifled muskets, fought off the assault. By the time that the Union infantry arrived, the Confederates had established a formidable defensive line that discouraged attack. Most of Meade's corps commanders cautioned against an assault. A golden opportunity had slipped away, and so did Lee's army. Although the Confederates had suffered a major defeat at Gettysburg, they had completed perhaps the most successful foraging expedition of the war. Robert E. Lee could thank his black teamsters for that.[55]

Notes

1. Jacob Hoke, *The Great Invasion of 1863* (Dayton, OH: Shuey, 1887; reprint, New York: Yoseloff, 1959), 107–8. The Hoke quote is taken almost verbatim from Charles Hartman Diary, June 22, P. Schaff Library, Lancaster Theological Seminary.

2. Philip Schaff, "Gettysburg Week," *Scribners Magazine* 16:24.

3. Schaff, "Gettysburg Week," 25.

4. Rachel Cormany Diary, June 16, 1863, Letters and Diaries, Franklin County, Pennsylvania, "Valley of the Shadow: Two Communities in the American Civil War," Virginia Center for Digital History, University of Virginia (http://valley.vcdh.virginia.edu), hereafter cited as "Valley."

5. Reverend Thomas Creig Diary, June 26, 1863, Valley.

6. William Heyser Diary, June 18, 1863, Valley; *Franklin Reporter*, July 8, 1863, 1; Ted Alexander, "A Regular Slave Hunt," *North and South* 4 (September 2001): 7, quoting Jemima K. Cree letter, Kittochtinny Papers, 1905–1908 (Chambersburg, PA: 1908), 94.

7. Sarah Sites Rodgers, *The Ties of the Past: The Gettysburg Diaries of Salome Myers Stewart, 1854–1922* (Gettysburg, PA: Thomas, 1996), 145.

8. Tillie Pierce Alleman, *At Gettysburg; or, What a Little Girl Saw and Heard of the Battle* (New York: W. Lake Borland, 1889), 19.

9. Mary Elizabeth Montfort, "How a Twelve-Year-Old Girl Saw Gettysburg," Montfort file, ACHS.

10. Peter C. Vermilyea, "The Effect of the Confederate Invasion of Pennsylvania on Gettysburg's African American Community," *The Gettysburg Magazine* 24 (January 2001), 119, from interview with Jean Odom, April 13, 1994; for a study of the Yellow Hill community, see Debra Sandoe McCauslin, *Reconstructing the Past: Puzzle of the Lost Community at Yellow Hill* (Gettysburg, PA: For the Cause, 2007).

11. Mary Warren Fasnacht, *Memories of the Battle of Gettysburg, Year 1863* (New York: Princely Press, 1941), 3.

12. Fanny J. Buehler, *Recollections of the Rebel Invasion of One Woman's Experiences during the Battle of Gettysburg* (Gettysburg, PA: Star and Sentinel, 1896); obituary,

Basil Biggs, *Gettysburg Compiler*, June 13, 1906, Biggs File, ACHS; Vermilyea, "The Effect of the Confederate Invasion," 118–119.

13. Charles H. Glatfelter, *A Salutary Influence: Gettysburg College 1832–1985* (Gettysburg, PA: Gettysburg College, 1987), 184.

14. Buehler, *Recollections of the Rebel Invasion*, 11; Harry Matthews Bradshaw, *Re-visiting the Battle of Gettysburg: The Presence of African Americans before and after the Conflict* (Oneonta, NY: Matthews, 2001), 6.

15. Matthews, *Re-visiting*, 6, from "An Incident of the Battle of Gettysburg," *The Anglo-African*, December 26, 1863.

16. Clifton Johnson, *Battleground Adventures* (Boston: Houghton Mifflin, 1916), 192–93.

17. Johnson, *Battleground Adventures*, 182–83.

18. Vermilyea, "The Effect of the Confederate Invasion," 120, from T. W. Herbert, ed., "In Occupied Pennsylvania," *Georgia Review* (summer 1950): 104–5.

19. Johnson, *Battleground Adventures*, 189.

20. Jacob Hoke, *Historical Reminiscences of the War: In and about Chambersburg during the War of the Rebellion* (Chambersburg, PA: 1884), 38; Jemima K. Cree letter, Kittochtinny Papers, 1905–1908 (Chambersburg, PA: 1908), 94, both quoted in Ted Alexander, "A Regular Slave Hunt," *North & South* 4, no. 7 (September 2001): 85.

21. W. P. Conrad and Ted Alexander, *When War Passed This Way* (Greencastle, PA: Greencastle Bicentennial, 1982), 135–36, 149, from Charles Hartman Diary, 1863, Philip Schaff Library, Lutheran Theological Seminary; M. Jacobs, "Notes on the Rebel Invasion of Maryland and Pennsylvania and the Battle of Gettysburg," *Pilot*, July 28, 1863, 3–5; Hoke, *Great Invasion*, 96, 108–9, 111–13; *New York Herald*, June 20, 1862; Wilbur S. Nye, *Here Come the Rebels!* (Baton Rouge: Louisiana State University Press, 1965), 144–45, 252, 255; *Mercerburg Journal*, July 17, 1863; Alexander, "A Regular Slave Hunt," 86–87.

22. *Franklin Repository*, July 8, 1863, 1, Valley; C. K. Leach to his wife, July 16, 1863, quoted in Alexander, "A Regular Slave Hunt," 87.

23. *Mercerburg Journal*, July 17, 1863, from Alexander, "A Regular Slave Hunt," 86; OR, 2nd ser., vol. 7, 1145, and vol. 6, 705; Alexander, "A Regular Slave Hunt," 89n.

24. Jemima Cree letter, from Alexander, "A Regular Slave Hunt," 85; OR, 2nd ser., vol. 2, pt. 2, 732–33; Edwin B. Coddington, *The Gettysburg Campaign: A Study in Command* (New York: Scribner's, 1968), 161.

25. Truman Nelson, *The Old Man: John Brown at Harper's Ferry* (Toronto: Holt, Reinhart and Winston of Canada, 1973), 25–65; *Valley Spirit*, April 29, 1863; *Valley of the Shadow*, Franklin County, Pennsylvania, newspapers; also, Franklin County Christy Letters; William A. Frassanito, *Early Photography at Gettysburg* (Gettysburg, PA: Thomas, 1995), 110.

26. David Wills to Andrew G. Curtin, June 15, 1863; Andrew G. Curtin to David Wills, June 15, 1863; Military Dispatch Books, box 18, RG19.181, discovered by Timothy Smith in Pennsylvania State Archives.

27. Recruiting poster, June 1863, Gladstone 109, from Library Company of Philadelphia.

28. Ebenezer D. Bassett to Alexander Henry, June 16, 1863, Leon Gardiner Collection, Historical Society of Pennsylvania, Philadelphia, and Alexander Henry Papers, Philadelphia Union League Archives, both quoted in James Elton Johnson, "A History of Camp William Penn and Its Black Troops in the Civil War, 1863–1865," PhD dissertation, University of Pennsylvania, 1999, 30–31; Daniel R. Biddle and Murray Dubin, *Tasting Freedom: Octavius Catto and the Battle for Equality in Civil War America* (Philadelphia: Temple University Press, 2010), 289, 292.

29. Alexander Henry Papers, Historical Society of Pennsylvania, quoted in Johnson, "Camp William Penn," 32; Frank H. Taylor, *Philadelphia in the Civil War 1861–1865* (Philadelphia, 1913), 188, 243, 351; James M. Paradis, *Strike the Blow for Freedom: The Sixth United States Colored Infantry in the Civil War* (Shippensburg, PA: White Mane Books, 1998), 8–10; Harry C. Silcox, "Nineteenth Century Philadelphia Black Militant: Octavius V. Catto (1839–1871)," *Pennsylvania History* 44, no. 1 (January 1977), 59; *Public Ledger* (Philadelphia), June 18, 1863; June 19, 1; June 20, 1; Frederick M. Binder, "Pennsylvania Negro Regiments in the Civil War," *Journal of Negro History* 37 (October 1952): 386–88; *The* (Philadelphia) *Press*, June 25, 1863, 2; Stanton to Stearns, OR, 1st ser., vol. 27, pt. 3, 203.

30. Russell F. Weigley, "Emergency Troops in the Gettysburg Campaign," *Pennsylvania History*, 25, no. 1 (January 1958): 39–57; OR, 1st ser., vol. 27, pt. 2, 211–12; Nye, *Here Come the Rebels!*, 224–25, 228, 232, 299, 339.

31. *The Philadelphia Inquirer*, June 26, 1863; George F. Nagle, *The Year of Jubilee: Men of Muscle* (Harrisburg, PA: Nagle, 2010), 2:344, 346, 391, 400; *Daily* (Harrisburg) *Telegraph*, June 9, 1863.

32. Nagle, *The Year of Jubilee*, 391, 392, 394, 401; "General Orders No. 42," *Daily Telegraph*, June 15, 1863.

33. *Harrisburg Patriot and Union*, June 16, June 19, July 3, 1863; Nagle, *The Year of Jubilee*, 420, 425, 428–29, 442, 447, 454; *New York Herald*, June 26, 1863.

34. *Harrisburg Daily Telegraph*, June 25, 1863; Nagle, *The Year of Jubilee*, 455, 454, 468–70, 486–88.

35. Nagle, *The Year of Jubilee*, 502, 517–19, 520–21; Margaret S. Creighton, *The Colors of Courage: Gettysburg's Hidden History: Immigrants, Women, and African-Americans in the Civil War's Defining Battle* (New York: Basic, 2005), 153.

36. Scott L. Mingus, *Flames beyond Gettysburg: The Gordon Expedition June 1863: A History and Tour Guide* (Columbus, OH: Ironclad, 2009), 41–42, 45–47, 52.

37. Mingus, *Flames beyond Gettysburg*, 266, 276, 563n33, 298, 308, 311, 317.

38. OR, 1st ser., vol. 27, pt. 2, 277–79; Noah A. Trudeau, *Like Men of War: Black Troops in the Civil War, 1862–1865* (Boston: Little, Brown, 1998), 94–97; Nye, *Here Come the Rebels!*, 283–94; Gladstone, 166; Mingus, *Flames beyond Gettysburg*, 571–72n29, 342, 348, 350–51, 356, 357, 397, 572n29, 35; *Lancaster Weekly Express*, July 4, 1863, *Daily* (Lancaster) *Evening Express*, June 29, 30, 1863.

39. Mingus, *Flames beyond Gettysburg*, 351; OR, 1st ser., vol. 27, pt. 1, 467.

40. OR, 1st ser., vol. 27, pt. 2, 279.

41. William S. McFeeley, *Frederick Douglass* (New York: Norton, 1955). For a less favorable assessment (by the same scholar) of Howard's effectiveness as director of the Freedmen's Bureau, see McFeeley, *Yankee Stepfather: General O. O. Howard and the Freedmen* (New York: Norton, 1968); Creighton, *The Colors of Courage*, 280n63.

42. Mark M. Boatner III, *The Civil War Dictionary* (New York: McKay, 1959), 447–48.

43. Richard Rollins, "Black Confederates at Gettysburg," *Gettysburg Magazine* 6 (January 1, 1992): 96; also published in Richard Rollins, ed., *Black Southerners in Grey: Essays on Afro-Americans in Confederate Armies* (Redondo Beach, CA: Rank and File, 1994), 133.

44. Trudeau, *Like Men of War*, 63–83, 87–88; Dudley T. Cornish, *The Sable Arm: Negro Troops in the Union Army* (New York: Longmans Green, 1956; reprint, Lawrence: University Press of Kansas, 1987), 152–56.

45. Boatner, *The Civil War Dictionary*, 64–65; Patricia L. Faust, ed., *Historical Times Illustrated Encyclopedia of the Civil War* (New York: Harper & Row, 1986), 61; Stewart Sifakis, *Who Was Who in the Civil War* (New York: Facts on File, 1988), 55–56; William A. Frassanito, *Gettysburg: A Journey in Time* (New York: Scribner's, 1975), 195–97, 198–215; Harry W. Pfanz, *Gettysburg: The Second Day* (Chapel Hill: University of North Carolina Press, 1987), 173–79, 181, 247.

46. Pfanz, *Second Day*, 208, 209, 230; Harry Bradshaw Matthews, *Whence They Came: Families of United States Colored Troops in Gettysburg, Pennsylvania, 1815–1871* (privately published, 1992), 197.

47. Pfanz, *Second Day*, 98, 253, 309, 326; Vermilyea, "The Effect of the Confederate Invasion," 121–123; Gettysburg National Military Park, Vertical File 14-CF, 110.

48. Vermilyea, "The Effect of the Confederate Invasion," 113; Gettysburg National Military Park, Vertical File I-110, "Abraham Brien Farm."

49. U.S. Army Military History Institute, Carlisle, Pennsylvania, Gettysburg Civilian Files, "Bryan Farm."

50. Matthews, *Whence*, 95–96; Gettysburg National Military Park Vertical Files, Government Claims; Creighton, *The Colors of Courage*, 152.

51. J. David Petruzzi, www.bufordsboys.com.

52. *Veteran Licensed Battlefield Guide*; Gary Kross shared this guide story, long held as an oral tradition.

53. Report of Brigadier General Robert O. Tyler, OR, 1st ser., vol. 27, pt. 1, 872–74.

54. This segment on Lee's retreat includes much information from Kent Masterson Brown, "Retreat and Pursuit," lecture, Gettysburg College Civil War Institute, June 23, 2003, as well as from his book *Retreat from Gettysburg: Lee, Logistics, and the Pennsylvania Campaign* (Chapel Hill: University of North Carolina Press, 2005). His research included quartermaster records from the Army of Northern Virginia. Other sources on the retreat and pursuit include John W. Schildt, *Roads from Gettysburg* (Shippensburg, PA: White Mane, 1998); Ted Alexander, "Ten Days in July: The Pursuit to the Potomac,"

North & South 2, no. 6; Coddington, *The Gettysburg Campaign*, 535–74, as well as a tour of the route with Edwin C. Bearss.

55. Kent Masterson Brown lecture; Edwin C. Bearss, "Tour of Retreat and Pursuit Route," Gettysburg College Civil War Institute, June 24, 2003; Coddington, *The Gettysburg Campaign*, 530, 819n; Fitzgerald Ross, *Cities and Camps of the Confederate States* (Champaign: University of Illinois Press, 1958), 65–66.

1. Margaret "Mag" Palm, demonstrating how her hands were bound in an attempt to kidnap her. Courtesy of Adams County Historical Society.

2. Basil Biggs, farmer and veterinarian, with his wife. Courtesy of Adams County Historical Society.

3. John "Jack" Hopkins acted as conductor on the Underground Railroad while caring for the buildings and grounds of Pennsylvania (later Gettysburg) College. Courtesy of Special Collections, Musselman Library, Gettysburg College.

4. Daniel Alexander Payne, student at Gettysburg's Lutheran Theological Seminary and teacher to the town's black community. Reverend Payne went on to become a bishop in the African Methodist Episcopal church and president of Wilberforce University. Used with permission from the Methodist Collection at Drew University library, Madison, New Jersey.

5. Lloyd F. A. Watts, educator and veteran of the Twenty-fourth Regiment of U.S. Colored Infantry. Courtesy of Jean Odom.

6. Lydia Hamilton Smith, humanitarian and confidante of Senator Thaddeus Stevens. Courtesy of LancasterHistory.org, Lancaster, Pennsylvania.

7. In Gettysburg's Dobbin House, a sliding shelf along the stairway conceals a space that local legend claims hid fugitive slaves. Courtesy of the author.

8. James Warfield lived in the original stone section of this house. Warfield's farm and blacksmith shop stood west of the famous Sherfey Peach Orchard on the Gettysburg Battlefield. Courtesy of the author.

9. McAllister Mill, active station on the Underground Railroad. Courtesy of the National Archives.

10. McAllister Mill from another angle. Only the foundation of the building remains. Courtesy of the National Archives.

11. "Cave" on Culp's Hill. The fallen tree trunk lies between the two halves of a split rock that may have served as a hiding place on the Underground Railroad. Courtesy of the author.

12. "Cave" on Culp's Hill, looking uphill. The split rock stands at the right center. The Culp's Hill observation tower in the upper left indicates the cave's location. Courtesy of the author.

13. South Washington Street. In 1863, Gettysburg's black community centered on these several blocks. During the battle, both Union and Confederate troops marched up and down this street. Courtesy of MOLLUS, U.S. Army Military History Institute, Carlisle, Pennsylvania.

14. On South Washington Street today, some buildings still bear scars of the battle. Courtesy of the author.

15. The Bryan farm, 1863. The farm of Abraham Brien ("Bryan" is a postwar spelling) rested by the focal point of Pickett's Charge. Courtesy of Library of Congress.

16. The Bryan house and barn today. Courtesy of the author.

17. Driving teams of mules was a difficult task indeed, as shown by this drawing in a veteran's memoir. Illustration by J. R. Chapin from the 1890 book by Civil War veteran Warren Lee Goss, *Recollections of a Private.*

18. Some of the tens of thousands of black teamsters who supplied both armies at Gettysburg. Courtesy of Library of Congress.

19. Columbia-Wrightsville Bridge. From the collection of York County Heritage Trust, York, Pennsylvania.

20. In this reproduction of a Bradley Schmehl color print, smoke and flames arise from the massive Columbia-Wrightsville Bridge over the Susquehanna River. Pennsylvania militia destroyed the bridge to stop the Confederate advance. Copyright Bradley Schmehl.

21. Camp William Penn in 1863, before wooden barracks were erected. Courtesy of Library of Congress.

22. U.S. Colored Troops in review at Camp William Penn. Of the eleven black regiments raised and trained here, ten included men from Gettysburg and its vicinity. Courtesy of National Archives.

23. Bodies of Union soldiers killed in the Gettysburg Campaign were exhumed from their original burial site in Hanover, Pennsylvania, between October 1863 and March 1864 for reburial in the Gettysburg National Cemetery. Samuel Weaver, the bearded man on the right, supervised this part of the operation. One of the four black men in the photo is probably subcontractor Basil Biggs of Gettysburg. The photograph was taken by Weaver's son, Peter S. Weaver. Courtesy of Gettysburg National Military Park Archives.

24. Lincoln Cemetery includes the graves of Abraham Brien, Lloyd F. Watts, and some thirty other black Civil War veterans. Courtesy of the author.

25. Abraham Lincoln with William H. Johnson, valet and bodyguard. LP512, "Lincoln Arrives in Baltimore." Courtesy of the Abraham Lincoln Presidential Library and Museum.

26. Dr. Alexander T. Augusta, Union surgeon, with rank of major. At the end of the Civil War, he was promoted to lieutenant colonel, the first African American to attain that rank. Courtesy of the Oblate Sisters of Providence Archives, Baltimore, Maryland.

27. The labor of many black workers helped create the Gettysburg National Military Park. Years later, this work crew from a nearby camp of the Civilian Conservation Corps maintained and enhanced the park during the Great Depression years. This photo was taken near the south boundary of the park on the Emmitsburg Road, circa 1937. Courtesy of Gettysburg National Military Park Archives.

28. Black Civil War veterans were not invited to the 1913 fiftieth anniversary reunion at Gettysburg, although African Americans like this porter did much of the work preparing and running the event. Courtesy of National Archives.

29. By the seventy-fifth anniversary reunion in 1938, black veterans, such as the one seated in the foreground in this tent event, had begun to take the places that they had earned. Courtesy of Gettysburg National Military Park Archives.

30. This unidentified black veteran, bearing a medal and perhaps accompanied by his son, attends the seventy-fifth anniversary event. Courtesy of Gettysburg National Military Park Archives.

31. This veteran, identified as C. T. Budd of Birmingham, Alabama, also attended the seventy-fifth anniversary events at Gettysburg in 1938. Courtesy of Gettysburg National Military Park Archives.

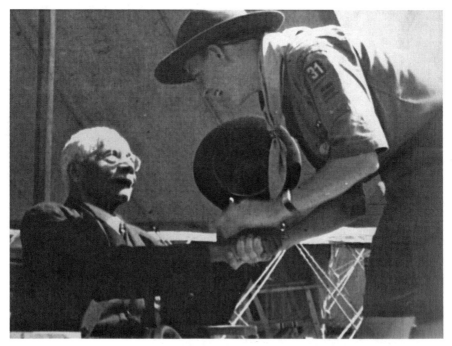

32. Veteran Thomas Waters with Boy Scout. Courtesy of Gettysburg National Military Park Archives.

CHAPTER FOUR

~

In the Wake of the Storm

Recalling the field of battle after a horrendous day of fighting at Gettysburg, Col. E. P. Alexander remembered that his "faithful" servant Charlie "came up hunting for me, with a fresh horse, affectionate congratulations on my safety, and, what was equally acceptable, something to eat." He went on to recall, "Negro servants hunting for their masters were a feature of the landscape that night." Some of the wounded Confederate officers might have been left behind if their servants had not taken upon themselves the job of overseeing their evacuation. Lt. James Mincy was one wounded officer who was designated to be left behind. Rube, his servant, was not about to let that happen. He somehow stole a horse and wagon and took personal charge of evacuating Mincy.

Lt. Col. Wharton J. Green's servant Guilford similarly drove an "impressed" buggy carrying Green and another wounded officer. Henry Johnson, who functioned both as servant and barber, helped Lt. Col. Benjamin F. Carter into an ambulance. A servant named Edmund took a horse from a wounded cavalryman so that his master, Captain W. A. Graham, could ride away on the retreat, but Graham was unable to ride. The servant was able to flag down an ambulance, however, and both of them managed to get a space on board.

Not only officers had servants to aid them. Noncommissioned officers such as Sgt. Maj. C. C. Cumming of the Seventeenth Mississippi brought servants with them as well. Cumming's servant George found an ambulance for him when he was wounded. After jostling violently over the rutted roads, many wounded Confederates could not bear to continue the torturous retreat. Many, including Cumming, asked to be left behind rather than to endure the agony of the wagon ride. Around Cashtown, the ambulance came to a halt. George lifted the sergeant from the ambulance and carried him to a barn near the road where dozens of other wounded would end their retreat.

Some wounded did not survive the evacuation. On the afternoon of July 5, Major Donald McLeod of the Eighth South Carolina died while being transported. His servant pulled the lifeless body from the ambulance. He buried the remains in a "beautiful grove" nearby and personally marked the grave, fashioning a headboard bearing the initials of the man who in life claimed to own him. Determined to see his task through to the end, the faithful servant rejoined the retreating army and continued on to South Carolina to inform the McLeod family of Donald's fate. The major's widow, distraught over his death, asked for his remains to be brought home. A year after the war, the nameless slave led a pair of men back to the grove that had become a gravesite. They exhumed the remains for the journey home.

When servants searched the battlefields for missing masters, they often found a corpse. Col. Isaac E. Avery led an unsuccessful attack on the Union right at East Cemetery Hill, but he did not return with his brigade when it was driven back. Avery's servant Elijah recovered the body and took personal responsibility for trying to return his remains to his home in Western North Carolina. Elijah carried the body to a quartermaster wagon for the sad journey home. By the time they reached the Potomac crossing at Williamsport, however, the summer heat had made it necessary for Elijah to bury his master there alongside others who had died on the retreat. When Col. Henry King Burgwyn Jr. of the Twenty-sixth North Carolina was killed and buried on the outskirts of Gettysburg, his mournful servant Kincheon could not accept his death. He gathered himself, however, and began a journey home with Burgwyn's two horses and clothing to bring back to the colonel's parents. The quartermaster who sent him on his way with ninety-five dollars trusted with certainty that, in spite of the temptations presented by the money and the two horses, he would do what he saw as his duty. He commented, "I never saw fidelity stronger in anyone." Kincheon completed the sad journey, alternately riding and walking.

During the retreat, some Confederate officers became casualties in skir-mishes with Federal cavalry. Black servants accompanied some of these men as well. Brig. Gen. James J. Pettigrew had been wounded in the hand while leading the left of Pickett's Charge. During the retreat, his unit protected the rear of Lee's army as it crossed the Potomac at Falling Waters. With Pet-tigrew traveled his servant Peter, whom he had known from his North Carolina youth. They had traveled the road of war together from its beginning. Peter rode beside the general, and as a firefight broke out at Falling Waters, he had to watch helplessly as his companion was shot. Peter and Pettigrew's staff hastened to the general's side and carried the mortally wounded man away from the fighting. After crossing into Virginia, the general died with Peter trying to the end to comfort him. Peter joined the officers who brought the general's body home.[1]

Wayland Fuller Dunaway maintained a close relationship with Charles Wesley. He explains his unusual relationship in his *Reminiscences of a Rebel*:

> There was one man that should have been mentioned before this time,—a negro of my own age, whose name was Charles Wesley. We had grown up on the farm together, and had played, and boxed, and wrestled without respect to color. Not as a slave but as a friend he followed me to the war,– my launderer, my cook, and when I was sick, my nurse. Having orders to keep himself out of danger, he very willingly remained far in the rear when a battle was in progress, but when the firing ceased he faithfully sought me and reported for duty. While writing about Charles, I may anticipate a little and say that when we were in Pennsylvania I told him that we were on Yankee soil, and that he had the opportunity of deserting me and of remaining there as a free man. He replied that he already knew that, but that he was going to abide with me. And when I was captured at Falling Waters he had the intelligence and fidelity to ride my horse home and deliver him to my brother.

The letters of Edgeworth Bird, a quartermaster for a Georgia Regiment in John Bell Hood's Division, illustrate a complex relationship between some slave owners and the people they claimed as property. Bird brought his servant Sam with him when he went off to war. Apparently, he had a second servant whom he shared with an officer who had none. Bird depended greatly on Sam. He said of him, "He is our only dependence now, Charlie is with Captain Smith. If he should be taken now, we'd be afoot." When Sam became seriously ill, however, Bird sent him back to the plantation to recover. He admitted to having a difficult time without his helper:

> I am gratified to hear Sam is so true to me and to his Regiment. I miss him very much, and should be a great deal more comfortable, could I have his services. No one washes or cooks like Sam here. Indeed, I do without many comforts I should have, were he here to call on. If he is entirely well, I should like to have him come on with Captain Smith.

The quartermaster anxiously wrote home inquiring about Sam's health and when he would return. In one letter to his wife, he requested that she "ask him when he thinks his furlough will expire." With Sam still incapacitated in 1863, Bird admitted that he could not get along without a servant and sent for another, Robert, to take his place. Robert's wife, Nancy, was literate in spite of laws forbidding teaching blacks to write. In a surprising letter, Bird writes, "Bob was in high glee over his letter from Nancy. Tell her to send him more." The Confederate officer not only allowed flouting the law against black literacy but actively encouraged it.

Eventually, many Southerners faced what historian Eugene Genovese called "the moment of truth." Some black servants chose not to stay with their masters. Confederate general Joseph Johnston had to admit that "we never have been able to keep the impressed Negroes with an army near the enemy. They desert." Slave owners may have wondered, Genovese thought, "Could it be that they had never known 'their people' at all? That they had been deceiving themselves?" He goes on to point out, "The masters had expected more than obedience from their slaves; they had expected faithfulness—obedience internalized as duty, respect, and love." This belief was necessary for slaveholders to see themselves as benign.

One planter wrote after the war,

> The conduct of the Negro in the late crisis of our affairs has convinced me that we were all laboring under a delusion. . . . I believed that those people were content, happy, and attached to their masters. But events and reflection have caused me to change these opinions; . . . If they were content, happy, and attached to their masters, why did they desert him in the moment of his need and flock to an enemy, whom they did not know; and thus left their, perhaps really good masters whom they did know from infancy?

The moment of truth may have come for Edgerton Bird in the Gettysburg Campaign. Although many black servants showed loyalty to the people who claimed to be their masters, this surely did not mean that those blacks accompanying the Confederate army accepted the status of slave. Often what appeared to be loyalty on the part of those who were enslaved was not loyalty so much as self-preservation. Many blacks took advantage of being in the free state of Pennsylvania to seize their freedom. Bird said it plainly, "A great many Negroes have gone over to the Yankees. Antony, Waddell's boy, has." One Pennsylvania resident commented to a Southern forager, "Your negroes run to us a little more willingly than our horses run to you." In fact, when Pennsylvania civilians reported seeing blacks held as captives, many of those captives were not kidnapped Pennsylvanians but teamsters, laborers, or servants accompanying the Army of Northern Virginia who had been captured in their unsuccessful flight for freedom.

Black servants had a perspective clearly different from that of white Southerners. During the retreat through Pennsylvania, Southern soldiers either spoke confidently of victory to Northern residents or remained silent. Only the black servants would reveal that the Confederates had been badly whipped.

Some who escaped slavery did so in a well-planned fashion. Captain Charles F. Waddell, after a brief absence from his Twelfth Virginia Regiment, returned to his unit planning to bivouac. Not only did his slave Willis not set up camp, but he had decided that he would not be a slave and ran off with all of the captain's camping gear.[2]

African Americans in the Medical Service

Some blacks were among the first to respond to the wounded on the field, such as Zanzibar-born Frederic Capron (see Appendix A). An unknown number of African Americans helped with hospital efforts after Gettysburg. The surgeon of the Third Pennsylvania Cavalry, Dr. Theodore T. Tate, hired African American Nelson Royer as a servant during the winter of 1862. Throughout the battle, Royer accompanied the surgeon. In the bloody aftermath of the battle, he assisted Tate at a hospital set up at the public school on East High Street. Later Royer enlisted in the Twenty-fifth Regiment of U.S. Colored Infantry. In a letter written twenty years after the battle, "Dr. T. T. Tate, Physician & Surgeon, West Middle St." wrote:

> When I was a surgeon of the 3rd Pa. Cavalry in the winter of 1862 I picked up Nelson Royer some place in Virginia and hired him as a servant. He proved to be a good man and I kept him from that time until the Reg. was mustered out in August 1864. He was with me at the Battle of Gettysburg. I there took charge of a Hospital at this place and kept the old man with me. When I got orders to go to the front he went with me back, and I there kept as I said before until my Expiration of service, during this time I never knew him to be sick an hour.

Many other African Americans helped anonymously in the work of aiding the wounded and repairing the physical damages of war. They performed a broad spectrum of tasks, from working in the hospital kitchens to repairing the railroads. The task of restoring the railroad fell mostly to black laborers. By July 10, the tracks that had been torn up by the invaders were carrying thirty trains daily in and out of Gettysburg. Incoming trains brought desperately needed medical supplies and tents. Outgoing trains carried the wounded away to places such as Philadelphia for extended hospital care.[3]

African American men and women helped to treat the thousands of wounded in the "vast sea of misery" left by the great battle. They remain, for the most part, nameless, forgotten individuals. Thousands more would care anonymously for the wounded on other battlefields and in hospitals scattered all over the country.

Some blacks, however, served as surgeons during the Civil War. By the end of the war there would be at least twenty-three African American graduates of medical schools in the United States, a number of them serving the Union army by the time of the Battle of Gettysburg. Several blacks who had completed their medical training in other countries also served as surgeons or assistant surgeons during the war.

Army regulations assigned each regiment one surgeon and one or more assistant surgeons. Other surgeons and assistants were assigned to hospitals. Surgeons carried the rank of major, and assistant surgeons that of captain or first lieutenant. The army would also hire "contract surgeons" on an ad hoc basis. They would step in to treat the survivors after a major battle and leave after all had been treated. By 1863, though, contract surgeons had to commit to at least three months' service. The Civil War medical service included at least nine black contract surgeons.

In 1849, two African Americans, John DeGrasse and Thomas J. White, graduated from the Medical School of Maine, affiliated with Bowdoin College. Joshua Lawrence Chamberlain taught at Bowdoin; a colleague, Professor Calvin Stowe married Harriet Beecher, author of *Uncle Tom's Cabin*. Following graduation and two years of study in Paris, DeGrasse joined the Massachusetts Medical Society and successfully practiced medicine in that state. As soon as black regiments were authorized in 1863, he volunteered and secured a commission as assistant surgeon. At the time of the Battle of Gettysburg, DeGrasse's regiment was serving in South Carolina.

Even before the government authorized the formation of black regiments, at least one African American medical officer served in a white regiment. David O. McCord, graduate of Medical College of Ohio in Cincinnati, was commissioned assistant surgeon in the Sixty-sixth Illinois Infantry, although he actually spent his time working at a Freedmen's Hospital. Later he was promoted to surgeon and served as medical director and inspector of freedmen in the Department of Tennessee and in Arkansas.

Cortlandt van Rensselear Creed, the first African American to earn a degree from Yale, graduated from Yale University Medical School and joined a Connecticut regiment as acting assistant surgeon. Graduating from the Medical Department of Dartmouth College, William Ellis served in Washington, DC, as acting assistant surgeon.

John Rapier, graduating in 1863 from Iowa College of Physicians and Surgeons, was the first such graduate of his race west of the Mississippi. He became an acting assistant surgeon in the U.S. Colored Troops. Benjamin A. Boseman, another graduate from the Medical School of Maine, was appointed acting assistant surgeon in August 1864. He served in Hilton Head, South Carolina, and remained there after the war practicing medicine and serving in the state legislature. Joseph Dennis Harris studied at the Medical Department of Western Reserve College. He was appointed acting assistant surgeon in June 1864 and eventually took charge of Howard Grove Hospital for the Freedmen's Bureau in Portsmouth, Virginia.

Some medical professionals did not complete their training until after the fighting had ended. They served by helping to deal with the aftermath of the war, particularly by ministering to the thousands of sick and homeless refugees who were formerly enslaved.

Rebecca Lee, overcoming combined racial and gender discrimination, completed her medical training in 1864. As the war ended, she traveled to the fallen Confederate capital. There, she dedicated herself to caring for the destitute former slaves. She married another black doctor, Arthur Crumpler, and returned to Boston, concentrating on nutrition and preventative medicine. In 1883, she published a pioneering work on medical care for women and children, entitled *Book of Medical Discourses*. Charles Barleen Purvis studied at Oberlin College, the first college to accept black students, and completed medical training at Western Reserve. By the time he was free to enter the army, the Confederates had surrendered. He worked in the Freedmen's Hospital in Washington, DC, and later taught at Howard Medical College. At Howard Hospital, he served on the medical staff and as chief of surgery. After a fifty-four-year association with Howard, he died in 1930 at the age of 97.

Alexander Ruffin Abbott apprenticed with Dr. Alexander T. Augusta in Canada. He worked as acting assistant surgeon with the U.S. Colored Troops in Washington, DC, at Freedmen's Hospital. He returned to Canada to resume his practice, joined the College of Physicians and Surgeons of Ontario, and eventually became president of the Kent County Medical Society in Ontario.[4]

Major Martin Delaney is usually credited with being the first African American to achieve field command, commissioned major in March 1865. Before the war, Delaney had studied at Harvard Medical School until the protest of white students from the South pressured the administration to ask him and other black students to leave. He completed medical and dental training through apprenticeship. When the war came, however, Delaney's

main contribution was not medical but as an effective recruiter. His abolitionist activities had included publishing his own newspaper, as well as working with Frederick Douglass on his newspaper, the *North Star*. Working with
abolitionist John Brown, Delaney also chaired the Chatham Convention in
Canada, which created a constitution for the independent community that
John Brown intended to establish after his ill-fated raid on Harpers Ferry.

Alexander T. Augusta applied for and was granted a commission as surgeon of colored troops in April 4, 1863. Since being commissioned surgeon
brings the commensurate rank of major, this appointment made Augusta the
first African American to obtain this field rank, predating Delaney by almost
a year. Born free in 1825 in Norfolk, Virginia, Augusta learned to read and
write through the mentoring of Daniel Alexander Payne, who would years
later graduate from Gettysburg's Lutheran Theological Seminary. He applied
unsuccessfully to several U.S. medical schools and eventually enrolled in
Trinity College of Medicine of the University of Toronto. Completing his
training at Trinity, he applied for a commission and passed the medical examination. His two white assistants bristled at the thought of serving under
a black man, and to preserve the peace, he was detached to examine black
volunteers in Washington, DC.

In spite of his rank, Augusta received the same rate of pay as a colored private for more than a year. He served at several posts; most notably, he took
charge of a Federal hospital for colored troops in Savannah, Georgia. He
turned the hospital into a model facility, and his stellar performance earned
him a promotion to brevet lieutenant colonel after the war ended. This was
the highest rank attained by an African American at that time and for several decades to come. While wearing his officer uniform in Washington, DC,
he was denied a seat on the streetcar because of his race. Members of the U.S.
Congress were outraged enough about the incident to pass a law forbidding
racial discrimination on the city's streetcars. In 1866, when Howard Medical
College opened, he was the only black faculty member.[5]

Few of the blacks who served in Gettysburg hospitals received any recognition for their services, but one self-sacrificing volunteer became the subject
of a newspaper article:

> She was poor, yet had she a little money saved up, a trifle at a time, by years of
> labor. Her name was Lydia Smith. . . . She, from her penury, gave her mite to
> the cause of the suffering, and that mite was her all.
>
> From a white neighbor she hired a ramshackle wagon with which he did
> hauling, and a horse. The horse was a pile of bones, else, probably, it would not
> have been in Adams County at all, but mounted by a Confederate cavalryman.

Lydia circled widely through the farm section around Bendersville and York Springs, which had not been so utterly devastated as the region contiguous to Gettysburg. Eloquently she told of tens of thousands of suffering men:

"I thank de good Lawd that put it in my heart to try to do something for these poor Creatures."

Where she could get donations of delicacies and suitable clothing she accepted them. When donations failed she bought till she had spent the very last penny of her little hoard acquired by years of frugality and toil. But now the wagon was heaped high to its full capacity, and she turned toward the hospitals miles away. The old horse swayed and tottered, but Lydia walked by his side and led him on over dusty highways and rugged hills till, at length, the tents were at hand.

And then Lydia, feeling not the weariness from many miles of travel, began to distribute the articles she had brought—to Union Soldiers, of course?

No! Union and Confederate lay side by side; and that noble colored woman saw not in the latter the warriors who were striving to perpetuate the slavery of her race. She saw only suffering humanity: and to Union and Confederate alike was impartially given.[6]

The generosity of Gettysburg's citizens seems especially remarkable considering the damage and losses that they themselves had suffered. Whether white or black, people living on or near the battleground suffered damage to their homes and fences, food, livestock, and other personal property, taken or destroyed. While no black-owned buildings were used as hospitals, African Americans suffered their share of damage and hardship. When James Warfield returned to Seminary Ridge to survey the devastation of his home and shop, he found insult added to injury—fourteen fresh Confederate graves in his garden. Basil Biggs returned to his tenant house on the Crawford Farm and found that he had fared even worse. The Crawford house had been used as a Confederate hospital and forty-five Rebel graves surrounded his house. Not even the AME church cemetery was spared. Two Southern soldiers were buried there.

Basil Biggs, Abraham Brien, and James Warfield suffered some the worst financial losses in Gettysburg's black community. Biggs lost cows, cattle, and hogs, as well as forty-five acres of wheat. He assessed his total losses at $1,506.60. Brien lost two acres of barley and nearly five acres of wheat. The Union soldiers defending the area did extensive damage to his fences. Union horses had consumed a ton and a half of hay from Brien's barn.

John Hopkins's wife, Julia, carefully documented her losses. She filed a damage claim with the commonwealth for the items taken or destroyed by the Confederates. Her list included nineteen quilts, eight blankets, eleven comforts, five feather beds, five chaff beds, twenty yards of imported carpet, eighteen yards of rag carpet, a dozen china cups and saucers, eighteen plates, two rocking chairs, a copper kettle, four table cloths, thirty towels, two cooking glasses, two water bowls and pitchers, two large buckets, a coffee mill, a clock, a pair of shoes, three chickens, and a fat hog weighing 150 pounds. Her claim for property loss totaled $339.39. Even property hidden under the ground was not safe. She filed a separate claim of five dollars for the potatoes dug up from her garden.

Sophia Devan, who lived at the intersection of Taneytown and Emittsburg Roads, "lost doors, roofing, gardens, fences, beds, bedding, crockery, clocks, chairs, and tables." The trauma of this destruction and loss unnerved her to the point where she could not bear to live there and could not bring herself to return to her home for another year. When she did return, tragedy struck again. The widow received news that her young son Fleming, a volunteer with the U.S. Colored Troops, had been killed in battle.[7]

Burials

Some men might imagine that glory covers a battlefield, but no trace of that glory remains when the fighting is done. Just after the battle, General Meade commented, "I cannot delay to pick up the debris of the battlefield." That "debris" included thousands of bodies, human and equine, that covered the ground. The stench choked and nauseated those civilians and soldiers who remained. Ghastly sights assaulted the eyes. Dead horses and mules, some five thousand of them, were burned. The human dead, some eight thousand of them, lay in the July sun for days until soldiers and civilians, usually not volunteers, dug very shallow graves or simply threw dirt over the bodies where they had fallen on the field. The haphazard work meant that little or no identification of the bodies was carried out. The infernal landscape featured thousands of small earthen mounds, some with protruding arms or legs or even heads. The dead seemed to cry out for a decent burial.[8]

The task of reburying the Union dead from their shallow temporary "graves" to a permanent, proper burial site loomed as a challenging ordeal. The process would begin on October 27, 1863, and would not be completed until March 18 of the following year. Concerned government officials and other citizens laid ambitious plans for an impressive Soldiers' National Cemetery for the Union dead. But upon completion of the lofty planning, the grisly task of disinterment and reburial remained. The labor required strong backs and strong stomachs. Franklin W. Biesecker submitted the lowest bid for exhumation and reburial and thereby gained the contract, but black hands would do the dirty work. Biesecker hired Basil Biggs to do the bulk of the drudgery. It is possible that Biggs had decided to bid for the contract but knew that officials would be unlikely to favor a black man over white bidders. He may have asked Biesecker to bid on his behalf. A coworker, Leander Warren, described Biggs's task, which was as necessary as it was repulsive:

The dead that had been hastily buried after the battle were found in piles of 30 or 40 at some places where shallow ditches had been opened and the bodies tumbled in in almost any position. At one point near the angle of stone walls on the west slope of Culp's Hill we found 100 bodies at one point.

The bodies were in different states of preservation. Bodies that had been buried on high dry sections of the field were only skeletons when they were uncovered. But those that we found in low boggy places were heavy and six of them made a load for my father's horse.

One of the most difficult tasks was to try to identify all the bodies we found. In some instances we could tell only what army they belonged to by fragments of blue or gray uniforms that were found. Sometimes there were marks that would name the organization of which the dead had been a member and in many instances letters or other papers would give us the names and home addresses of the dead. At a number of places there were small board markers at the graves that had been placed by acquaintances of other persons who knew the identity of the soldier when he was buried. These boards were nailed to the top of the coffin. If we knew the names of the dead they were written across the lid of the coffin. When the bodies reached the cemetery, a careful record was made of all the information we had about each body and the resting place of each soldier.

. . . Basil Biggs, colored, of Gettysburg, was given the contract for disinterring the bodies on the field. He had a crew of eight or ten Negroes in his employ. Samuel Weaver directed Biggs' men and as each body was removed, Weaver went through the uniform pockets with an iron hook and sought for any means of identifying the body. Any papers or grave markers that he found were attached to the lid of the coffin and recorded when the body reached the cemetery.

. . . Biggs also had a man hauling coffins to the field and then to the cemetery. We worked every day that winter when it was fit. There wasn't much snow that year until after we had completed the work and there were few days that weather interferred [sic] with our task.

. . . While the work of uncovering the dead on the field was done by Negroes, the reburial at the national plot was in charge of white men.

. . . Biggs had a colored boy hauling with a team of two horses and he could haul nine coffins at a trip. I hauled only six. When the bodies were placed according to states in the cemetery, the men placed long signs over the graves indicating the state from which the soldiers had come. There were over 900 that were unknown and could not be identified in any way.[9]

Federal casualties of the campaign were not limited to the Gettysburg Battlefield. Union soldiers fought and died and were buried at other battle sites in the state. The soldiers buried in those towns and fields also had to be transferred to the new cemetery. In Hanover, Pennsylvania, for example, nineteen Union troops had been killed in a cavalry clash. At least eleven of them were disinterred at Hanover and moved to Gettysburg. A crew of African Americans performed this task. A local photographer captured them as they labored. Since the photograph is identified as "Samuel Weaver supervising the exhumation of Union dead in Hanover, Pa.," the black men in the photograph may be Basil Biggs and his work crew.[10]

When President Lincoln came to Gettysburg to deliver his dedication speech at the National Cemetery, Biggs was still at work. Burials would continue for four months after Lincoln had departed. Lincoln may have encountered some of Gettysburg's African American residents as soon as he stepped off the train at the Western Maryland Station. "Mag" Palm earned extra money by meeting the trains at this station and carrying the passengers' baggage for a fee of twenty-five cents. Certainly, Lincoln's audience at the dedication included people of color. The entire student body and staff of Pennsylvania College attended the ceremony; this probably included John Hopkins. The new cemetery, adjacent to the town's black neighborhood, surely drew a number of the nearby residents to the ceremony.

William H. Johnson, President Lincoln's personal valet, accompanied him to Gettysburg. Considering the widespread discrimination against people of color on public conveyances, Johnson could well have been the only black passenger on the train. Johnson's close relationship with Lincoln went back to their Illinois days. They had traveled together by train from Springfield to Washington, Johnson attentive to every need of the president-elect. His attentiveness to Lincoln indicated to observers that he served as an unofficial bodyguard. A reporter on the train observed Johnson's "untiring vigilance." The reporter judged that the valet was "the most useful member of the party." An assassination threat on the way to Washington made necessary a change in the travel route, intended to throw off any would-be assassins. Lincoln clandestinely changed trains at Baltimore, traveling with detective protection but with only one person from his Illinois entourage, William Johnson.

Lincoln expressed confidence in Johnson's "integrity and faithfulness." He judged the man to be "honest, faithful, sober, industrious, and handy as a servant" and as "a worthy man." The president naturally planned to place Johnson on the White House staff but was rebuffed by the existing staff. Johnson, besides being an "outsider," was dark-skinned, and the light-shinned White House staff shunned him.

Lincoln tried to help his friend obtain a position elsewhere in Washington. In the meantime, he gave Johnson a temporary job attending the White House furnace for fifty dollars per month. The chief executive sent out several letters of recommendation. One written to secretary of the navy Gideon Welles read,

> Dear Sir:
> The bearer (William) is a servant who has been with me for some time and in whom I have confidence as to his integrity and faithfulness. He wishes to enter your service. The difference of color between him and the other servants is the cause of our separation. If you can give him employment you will confer a favour on
> Yours truly,
> A. Lincoln

This intervention did not bear fruit, but a note to secretary of the treasury Salmon P. Chase resulted in Johnson's hiring as a laborer and messenger for the Treasury Department at a salary of six hundred dollars per year, a very good income for that time. His morning duties, however, took him to the White House, where he shaved the president, attended to his clothing, delivered messages, and probably continued to act as an informal bodyguard.

Not surprising, Lincoln took Johnson along with him on important trips. He accompanied Lincoln to another major battlefield site when the president paid a call on General McClellan, who still languished at the Antietam battlefield long after the fighting had ended and the enemy had withdrawn.[11]

The next year, in the wake of the Gettysburg Campaign, Lincoln received an invitation from David Wills of Gettysburg. Wills had helped to organize the creation of the new National Cemetery and plan the ceremony dedicating the site. In his invitation to the president, he explained, "It is the desire that you, as Chief Executive of the Nation, formally set apart these grounds to their sacred use by a few appropriate remarks." He would follow the chief speaker of the day, the renowned orator Edward Everett.

But this was a bad time for the First Family. Only a year earlier, the Lincolns had to bury their son Willie, who had died from typhoid fever. They had to watch helplessly as their son's life ebbed away. Abraham was distraught, Mary inconsolable. Now, as the date approached for the Gettysburg dedication ceremony, their other young son in the White House, Tad, became seriously afflicted with what could again become a fatal illness. Both parents felt great anxiety. Mary would certainly not leave her sick child to travel to Gettysburg. Her husband must have felt the need to stay as well.

Weighing heavily on his mind, though, was the death of so many soldiers and the importance of his message of rededication. He did not need the reminder in his invitation by Wills that "it will be a source of great gratification to the many widows and orphans that have been made almost friendless by the great battle here, to have you here personally." This feeling of obligation took precedence even over pressing demands of his family. He asked William to accompany him to Gettysburg.

They both stayed at the home of David Wills. Recalling the event years later, Wills, who also hosted Edward Everett, remembered, "I also invited the President to my house and he arrived there on the evening of the 18th of November, 1863. After spending part of the evening in the parlors he retired to his room. He had his colored servant, William, with him. Between nine and ten o'clock the President sent his servant to request me to come to his room. I went and found him with paper prepared to write." Obviously, Johnson was present as Lincoln put the finishing touches on his speech. Lincoln may have wanted to rehearse his address. If he did practice delivering his speech, the person most likely to have been in the room with him was William Johnson. This would mean that a black man could have been the first person to hear the Gettysburg Address.

Edward Everett would speak before Lincoln. In 1857, three years before President Lincoln's election, Everett had been asked by Peter Cooper to deliver an address at the inaugural meeting in the now-famous Cooper Union. He agreed to speak on condition that all of the proceeds from ticket sales would go to a fund at Everett's disposal, "to be appropriated to aid poor Charlotte Ashe, my old cook, in purchasing her daughter's freedom. The daughter is a slave in Mississippi, and Charlotte has for years been trying to effect this object." Bostonians responded generously.

The 1860 presidential election saw three other candidates vying against Lincoln. Everett accepted the vice presidential nomination as running mate of John Bell, the presidential nominee of the Constitutional Union Party. Everett publicly suppressed his antislavery views during the campaign to avoid alienating moderate voters. This infuriated other antislavery people and earned him the contempt of Republicans. At Gettysburg, he may have sought to redeem his image. While Lincoln never mentioned slavery or the Confederacy by name, Everett castigated both. He accused the Confederate states of attempting "to establish an oligarchy founded 'on the cornerstone of slavery.'" He also warned that submission to the Rebels would mean giving back to the South "the helpless Colored population, thousands of whom are periling their lives in the ranks of our armies, to a bondage rendered tenfold more bitter by the momentary enjoyment of Freedom."[12]

Lincoln's Gettysburg oration conveyed a message of special meaning to African Americans. Through this address, Lincoln helped to transform the American Civil War in a revolutionary way, from a war solely to restore the Union to one affirming the principles of freedom and equality. This brief speech redefined the meaning of the "great civil war," and in the process it redefined America and its people. According to Lincoln, the nation had been born "four score and seven years ago," when the Declaration of Independence (not the Constitution) was written. Unlike the Constitution, which accommodates slavery, the declaration presents as self-evident truth the proposition that all men are created equal and possess the unalienable right to liberty. The president also insisted that the nation had to have a "new birth of freedom" to ensure that those who had died there had not died in vain.

Conservative Northerners railed at the speech. To them, the speech insulted the memory of the men in blue who sacrificed their lives for the preservation of the Union, not for the equality of the races. But the war changed the way that many Americans thought about slavery and race relations. By his words at Gettysburg, Lincoln helped to nurture acceptance of that change.

While riding the train to Gettysburg, Lincoln had looked "careworn" to one observer. Throughout his visit to the town, he had looked very tired. On the return train, an excruciating headache knocked the president off his feet. The president was coming down with variola, a form of small pox. It had spread throughout Washington in the past year and had been especially deadly in the "contraband camps" that sheltered escaped slaves. Now it had reached the White House and took down two residents, Tad and Abraham Lincoln.

William Johnson attentively administered to the prostrated chief executive, cooling his burning forehead with cold water. He most likely continued caring for Lincoln when they returned to the White House. Lincoln and his son both recovered, but William Johnson, perhaps in ministering to the president's health, had imperiled his own. Small pox struck William Johnson virulently, requiring his hospitalization. A reporter visiting the White House dropped in on the president and found him counting out money and dividing it into labeled envelopes:

> I dropped in upon Mr. Lincoln on Monday last, and found him busily engaged in counting greenbacks, "This, sir," said he, "is something out of my usual line; but a President of the United States has a multiplicity of duties not specified in the Constitution, or acts of Congress: this is one of them. This money belongs

to a poor Negro, who is a porter in one of the departments (the Treasury). And who is at present very sick with the small pox. He is now in the hospital, and could not draw his pay, because he could not sign his name.

I have been at considerable trouble to overcome the difficulty, and to get it for him; and have at length succeeded in cutting red tape, as you newspaper men say. I am dividing the money, and putting a portion labeled in an envelope with my own hands, according to his wish;" and his Excellency proceeded to indorse the package very carefully.

Eventually, the man who had faithfully nursed the stricken president could not himself recover. He passed away from the small pox that he may have contracted from the president himself.

Lincoln took on the responsibility for Johnson's final needs. The chief executive himself paid all of the funeral and burial expenses. He arranged to have his loyal friend buried at Arlington Cemetery. Only a few years earlier, the Supreme Court had declared in the infamous *Dred Scott* decision that no black man can be a citizen of the United States. Lincoln provided a headstone reading simply,

William H. Johnson   Citizen[13]

Captured Southern Blacks

The thousands of Confederate personnel taken as prisoners included many African Americans. Their unique status is reflected in the conundrum faced by Federal officials in determining what to do with them. As early as July 30, 1863, the commanding officer of Fort McHenry Prison in Baltimore sent the following letter:

Head-Quarters, 2nd Separate Brigade, 8th Army Corps,
    Defences [sic] of Baltimore,
    Fort McHenry, Md., July 30th 1863.
    Lt Col Wm H. Cheeseborough
    Asst Adjt General
    Colonel
    I have the honor to inform you that sixty four (64) Negroes, Servants of Officers in the Rebel Army , have been received at this Post, from time to time, with the prisoner of war from Gettysburg and vicinity. Of this number sixteen (16) have enlisted in the Negro [Regiment] now in process of Organization in [Baltimore]—four (4) have been enlisted as Assist Cooks in Co D 5 N.Y. Artillery, now at this Post—four (4) left clandestinely with the 21st Reg-N.Y.

[Infantry]. National Guard, on its return to New-York, the balance, forty, are still here and chiefly employed in police duty.

I would respectfully suggest that the propriety of employing these forty men, in the Service of the Government as laborers, teamsters, &c&c. Some disposition of them is desirable

I am Colonel
Very respectfully
Your Obedt Servant
W.W. Morris
Bvt Brig Gnl Comdg

P.S. A few of those remaining here, mentioned above, are acting as officers servants and receive wages—a few others are free Negroes and have families to whom they desire to return.

On October 6, Col. P. A. Porter, colonel of the Eighth New York Volunteer Artillery, stationed at Fort McHenry, suggested a policy clarification in a letter to Col. William Hoffman, commissary general of prisoners:

You state that Captured Negroes are ranked as Camp followers, and therefore Prisoners of War.

It is respectfully suggested that they be employed in the service of the Government as paid laborers and teamsters—thus rendering service to the Government, and avoiding the return to slavery of such as were slaves. It is further suggested that those among them who are freed men with families and desire to go should be sent south with the first installment of prisoners going thither—as exchanged prisoners or not as the Government thinks best.

If the questions here raised are beyond your jurisdiction, it is respectfully asked that this communication be forwarded by you to the Secretary of War.

These questions of policy certainly stirred up some disagreement. One problem was the uncertainty of Northerners as to where the true loyalty of Southern blacks lay. Maj. Gen. E. W. Hitchcock revealed his suspicions when he declared,

I do not recommend that any colored men be sent South, for exchange, either with or against their will.

If there are any who wish to be discharged upon oath of allegiance I see no reason for refusing them the privilege of doing so.

If any *prefer* to go South, I would recommend their being detained as prisoners, but not prisoners of war, and would employ them or not as circumstances might render expedient.

A November 29 telegram from the War Department to Fort McHenry inquired, "In reference to the negroes servants of the Rebel officers, who have been captured from the enemy; wishes to know how many of them, there are left, and how employed." The post replied later that day:

> Thirty-two (32) Negro camp followers, captured from the enemy are accounted for at this post, viz:
> Sixteen (16) employed as servants, teamsters, &c. &c.
> Ten (10) enlisted as cooks in 5th N.Y. Vol. Arty.
> Six (6) escaped.

This report uses the expression "Negro camp followers *captured from the enemy*," rather than "captured enemy camp followers." This reveals the unique, ambiguous status of these prisoners: they are not the enemy; they are *taken from* the enemy. Colonel Porter went on to account for all of the black prisoners.

1. Soloman Dillon	at Fort McHenry in Prison Cook House	
2. Frederick Simms	"	"
3. Samuel Hanan [?]	"	Police duty
4. John Kane	"	"
5. Wm Burks	"	"
6. George Bird	"	"
7. Simeon Coons	"	"
8. Charles Scott	"	Teamster
9. Enos Ward	"	works for Capt Connor 8 N.Y.V.A.
10. Henry Clay	"	" " Lieut Cork 8 NYVA
11. Charles H. Lacey	West Building's Batteries	" " Lieut Nellis 5 NY
12. Richard Banter	Fort McHenry	" " Lieut Murray 5 NY
13. John Owens	"	" " Lieut Andrews 5 NY
14. George Norris	Fort McHenry	Lieut Rollin 5 NYA
15. Olmstead Owens	"	Lieut Andrews 5 NYA
16. John Oliver	"	Capt Cotter [?]
	Total	16

Enlisted in	Co F [?]	5th NYVA as Cooks	4
" "	Co D	5th NYVA as Cooks	4

"	"	Co A	5th NYVA as Cooks	2
		Total		12

Escaped		
John Petticord	More than two months ago	
John Luby	"	
John Ciane	"	
John Brown	"	
Philetus [?] Brown	"	
Washington Cozzens	(Nov 27 186) [sic]	6
	Total	6

Recapitulation	at Fort McHenry	16
	Enlisted	10
	Escaped	6
Total		32

The motivation of the six who escaped remains a mystery. Did they make their escape because they were truly loyal to the Confederate cause, or did they just long to go home?

The War Department finally established a clear policy on December 18, 1863:

> In relation to the question of the disposition which should be made of certain Negroes, who have been in the service of Rebel officers captured in battle and in company with them brought to your post . . . , the Secretary of War directs, that on no account can any colored men be sent South for Exchange, either with or against their will. Those who wish to take the oath of allegiance can be discharged, and if they so choose, continue as private servants of officers, or serve the Government as Cooks, Teamsters, Laborers or in any other capacity in which they can be useful.
>
> Those who refuse to take the oath of allegiance will be detained as prisoners of war, and will be employed or not, as the Commanding Officers of the Post where they are confined, may deem expedient and proper.[14]

Born on the Battlefield: A New Birth of Freedom

A compelling story has recently come to light. Victor Chambers has passed on the oral history of his mother's life in slavery and freedom. It includes a remarkable account of her escape and of his birth.

Victor's grandmother came to Philadelphia from Haiti in 1787, as did many others during the Haitian slave rebellion. She married and "went to live on a farm in the country," possibly in Delaware. They had a daughter,

Henrietta, but as a child in 1827 slave catchers kidnapped her and sold her into slavery in Virginia. There she lived the life of a slave on the Barksdale plantation. This Virginia Barksdale slave owner was a relative of the famous William Barksdale of Mississippi, who boldly led a brigade of Mississippi troops at Gettysburg. Henrietta had told her son, Victor, that she was "well acquainted with young Massa Will." She endured thirty-six years of slavery before making her escape to the North in 1863. Her advanced state of pregnancy at the time made her escape attempt all the more difficult.

She made her way to Gettysburg on June 30. Her flight was halted on July 1, however, by the fighting north of town where Union Major General John F. Reynolds was killed. She retreated to a safer location a little to the south but, unfortunately, that became the site of some of the fiercest fighting on the second day of the battle. In this area Confederate Brigadier General William Barksdale led his Mississippians in an assault that cost him his life.

Henrietta related to her son the ghastly scene of the battlefield as well as the circumstances of his birth.

> My mother could not get away from the field. After three days the fight was over, she wandered over the bloody field looking at the dead and wounded. I have heard her say many a time it was hell, hell. Once seen, *never* forgotten. Dead men, dead horses wounded and dying men wherever she went; she was giving a poor soldier a drink, and he died with the first swallow. I was born on the battlefield of Gettysburg on July 7, 1863, four days after the fight. I was born in an old army wagon that had all the wheels shot off it and the six mules were lying in the harnesses just as they had been killed. No Doctors, no marble slabs, no hot water, no medicine. No one but God and my mother.

He was born free on a battlefield of the war that ended slavery in the United States. Born only a few days after a major Union victory, perhaps for this reason he was named Victor. His name commemorates the double victory of Union triumph on the battlefield and of freedom prevailing over slavery.

The Emancipation Proclamation went into effect on January 1, 1863. The Proclamation declared free all of the slaves in the areas in rebellion. Some people, even some historians, argue inaccurately that the Emancipation Proclamation did not free a single slave. Both Henrietta and Victor belie this proposition. Before the Proclamation, all slaves were considered to be property. Even those slaves who escaped from Confederate states were considered to be property captured from the enemy. They were called "contraband," a term that only emphasized their status as chattel, not free men and women. Now that Henrietta escaped from the area in rebellion, she was "henceforth and forever free." A child was considered legally free or slave according to the condition of his mother. Victor, therefore, was born free. Legally the Emancipation Proclamation made them free. In reality, however, they were both free because of the courage and fortitude of a woman who risked everything for the precious reward of freedom for herself and her child.[15]

Notes

1. Edward Porter Alexander, "The Great Charge and Artillery Fighting at Gettysburg," in *Battles and Leaders of the Civil War*, ed. Robert U. Johnson and Clarence C. Buel (New York: Century, 1884–1888), 360; Kent Masterson Brown, *Retreat from Gettysburg: Lee, Logistics, and the Pennsylvania Campaign* (Chapel Hill: University of North Carolina Press, 2005), 50, 61, 98, 100 112, 114–16, 147, 157, 285, 340, 347, 372.

2. Wayland Fuller Dunaway, *Reminiscences of a Rebel* (New York: Neal, 1913); John Rosier, ed., *The Granite Farm Letters: The Civil War Correspondence of Edgeworth & Sallie Bird* (Athens: University of Georgia, 1988).

3. Capron letter, Gettysburg National Military Park (see Appendix A); Harry Bradshaw Matthews, *Whence They Came: Families of United States Colored Troops in Gettysburg, Pennsylvania, 1815–1871* (privately published, 1992), 95–96; Peter C. Vermilyea, "The Effect of the Confederate Invasion of Pennsylvania on Gettysburg's African American Community," *Gettysburg Magazine* 24 (January 2001): 123; Gregory Coco, *A Vast Sea of Misery* (Gettysburg, PA: Thomas, 1988); Vermilyea, "The Effect of the Confederate Invasion," 121–23, from pamphlet by Georgeanna Woolsey, "Three Weeks at Gettysburg, 1863," 18–20; Jack McLaughlin, *Gettysburg: The Long Encampment* (New York: Bonanza Books, 1963), 182.

4. Robert G. Slawson, prologue to *Change: African Americans in Medicine in the Civil War Era* (Frederick, MD: NMCWM Press, 2006), 7–10, 16–18, 28–29, 32–34, 35–40.

5. Osborne P. Anderson, "A Voice from Harpers Ferry," Boston, 1861, www.libraries.wvu.edu/theses/Attfield/HTML/voice.html; for Delany's plans for African Americans to leave the United States and establish a self-governing nation, see Cyril E. Griffith, *African Dream: Martin Delany and the Emergence of Pan-African Thought* (University Park: Pennsylvania State University Press, 1975); James H. Whyte, "Maryland's Negro Regiments," *Civil War Times Illustrated* 1, no. 4 (1962): 42; Slawson, prologue, 10, 14–17, 22–24, 30–32, 34–36, 40, 41.

6. J. Howard Wert, "Lydia Smith," *Harrisburg Telegraph*, August 6, 1907, Gettysburg Civilian Files, U.S. Army Military History Institute, Carlisle, PA.

7. Gettysburg National Military Park, Damage Claims, Vertical Files, 14-CF-8, Basil Biggs; Abraham Brien, 14-CF-14; James Warfield, 14-CF-110; Vermilyea, "The Effect of the Confederate Invasion," 123–24; Margaret S. Creighton, *The Colors of Courage: Gettysburg's Hidden History: Immigrants, Women, and African-Americans in the Civil War's Defining Battle* (New York: Basic, 2005), 152.

8. OR, 1st ser., vol. 27, 79; Garry Wills, *Lincoln at Gettysburg: The Words That Re-made America* (New York: Simon & Shuster, 1992), 20–21.

9. Jacob Melchoir Sheads, "Re-burial of Union Dead in the National Cemetery," from extensive quote by Leander Warren, Leander Warren File, ACHS. For other descriptions of the aftermath of the battle, see two books by Gregory Coco, *Strange and Blighted Land* (Gettysburg, PA: Thomas) and *Wasted Valor* (Gettysburg, PA: Thomas, 1990); and Gerald R. Bennett, *Days of Uncertainty and Dread: The Ordeal Endured by the Citizens of Gettysburg* (Camp Hill, PA: Bennett, 1994).

10. William A. Frassanito, *Early Photography at Gettysburg* (Gettysburg, PA: Thomas, 1995), 167–68.

11. Gabor Boritt, *The Gettysburg Gospel: The Lincoln Speech That Nobody Knows* (New York: Simon & Schuster, 2008), 53–54; John E. Washington, *They Knew Lincoln* (New York: Dutton, 1942), 128–30.

12. Boritt, *The Gettysburg Gospel*, 66, 83; Alan Nevins, *Ordeal of the Union*, 4 vols. (New York: Scribner's, 1947), 1:520, from Everett Diary, June 22, 1857, Everett Papers, New York; for complete text of Everett's oration, see Boritt, *The Gettysburg Gospel*, 207–33.

13. See Wills, *Lincoln at Gettysburg*, for a thorough exegesis of the Gettysburg Address. See also Boritt, *The Gettysburg Gospel*, 127–28, 170, for a careful analysis of the speech; Washington, *They Knew Lincoln*, 133–34.

14. National Archives RG 107: Records of the Office of the Secretary of War, Entry 32: Letters Received from the Commissary General of Prisoners (selected items).

15. Harriette Rinaldi, *Born at the Battlefield of Gettysburg: An African-American Family Saga* (Princeton: Markus Wiener Publishers, 2004), xxiii–xxiv, 1, 75–99.

CHAPTER FIVE

~

Carrying the Struggle on to Victory

As early as May 1863, a local citizen recorded an account of the earliest known black volunteers in Gettysburg. Eventually, over thirty African Americans from Gettysburg and the vicinity joined the United States Colored Troops (USCT). Black volunteers from Pennsylvania were organized at Philadelphia and trained at Camp William Penn, just outside that city. All together, that camp would muster eleven regiments, over ten thousand black enlisted men and noncommissioned officers. Ten of those eleven regiments would include volunteers from the Gettysburg area. These were mostly volunteers, but as with white troops after 1863, some of them were called up by the draft or served as substitutes for a conscript.

The first regiment to complete its training at Camp William Penn was designated the Third Regiment of U.S. Colored Infantry (USCI). Its ranks included Francis Jackson and Samuel Stanton Sr., alias John Johnson. Other USCT regiments included the following:

Sixth USCI—Lindsay Jones
Eighth USCI—Isaac Buckmaster, Jonathan H. Buckmaster, Fleming Devan, William H. Devan, George W. Pennington, David A. Robinson, and John W. Watts
Twenty-second USCI—William Burley, Joseph Craig, Solomon Devan, John T. Redding, David J. Stevens, and Greenberrry Stanton
Twenty-fourth USCI—George Bolen, Emanuel Craig, Randolph Johnston and Lloyd F. Watts

Twenty-fifth USCI—Samuel Butler, Benjamin Craig, John Edward Hopkins, Nelson Royer, Alexander Scott, William Thompson, Joseph Turner

Thirty-second USCI—William Armstrong, Ennis Gaiter, William Jackson, Thomas McCullough, Alfred Monroe, Lewis Monroe, Richard Monroe, William Monroe, Elias Patrick, Harrison Rideout, Levi Rogers, Alexander Spriggs, and Lewis Spriggs

Forty-first USCI—John A. Disnick

Forty-third USCI—Robert W. Devan, Richard Myers, and Samuel A. Reed

127th USCI—Isaac Carter, Henry Gooden, Thomas Grigsby, Charles Hill, Isaac Madison, Samuel L. Matthews, Nelson E. Mathews, William H. Mathews, John W. Stanton, and George W. Wagner[1]

The combined military actions of these ten units spanned great geographic distance and included some of the most significant campaigns of the war. Although the Fifty-fourth Massachusetts included no Gettysburg residents, some seventeen residents of Chambersburg, Mercersburg, and surrounding Franklin County marched in its ranks. This regiment has become immortal through its fabled assault on Fort Wagner, near Charleston, South Carolina, and because of being center stage in the motion picture *Glory*, released in December 1989. Camp William Penn regiments, however, fought alongside the Fifty-fourth Regiment. The Third USCT finally captured Fort Wagner when the Confederates were forced to abandon it. The Eighth USCT fought side by side with the Fifty-fourth at Olustee, Florida, where they suffered horrendous casualties; many who were wounded and captured were executed by victorious Confederates. Those who were captured and survived suffered with the Fifty-fourth at the infamous prisoner-of-war camp at Andersonville, Georgia.[2]

In addition to direct combat, the war effort required a great number of troops for a variety of other functions. The Twenty-fourth USCT, sent to Point Lookout, Maryland, held the responsibility of guarding prisoners in the largest Northern prisoner-of-war camp. Many Confederates captured at Gettysburg would find themselves guarded by black citizen-soldiers from that Pennsylvania town. Sergeant Lloyd F. A. Watts, whose writing abilities contributed to his promotion, wrote home to his wife from the camp:

We are at Point Lookout in the state of Maryland. . . . It is a great looking place. There is nothing but water as far as your eyes can carry you. It is a narrow strip of land ninety miles from Baltimore and there is only one way to get out.

There are twenty-five thousand Rebels prisoners here we have to guard. It takes one hundred men for guard duty.[3]

Other Camp William Penn regiments took on garrison duty in occupied Southern towns. The Twenty-fifth USCI performed such duty in North Carolina, New Orleans, and Pensacola. The Thirty-second USCI assaulted entrenched infantry and artillery at Honey Hill, South Carolina, only to be repulsed. The regiment paid a heavy price, suffering sixty-four casualties, including Gettysburg's Lewis Spriggs, who was shot in the right foot. Later in the war, the Thirty-second Regiment participated in the siege of Charleston, South Carolina, and helped capture that cradle of secession.

In the spring of 1864, newly appointed general-in-chief Ulysses S. Grant sent Meade's Army of the Potomac against Lee's Army of Northern Virginia in a struggle of titans known as Grant's "overland campaign." About this time, the Forty-third USCT took the distinction of being the first black troops to be assigned to the Army of the Potomac. Throughout the Wilderness Campaign, the regiment provided support as part of the Ninth Corps.

The defiant Rebel capital of Richmond, Virginia, had fought off all previous Union threats. Grant devised an alternative approach for Richmond's capture. He would strike at Petersburg, a railroad center to the south. Capturing Petersburg would cut off Richmond's railroad lifelines. If Petersburg fell, Richmond would fall.

The first phase of this operation, the capture of Petersburg's outer works, fell to the Army of the James, which included a division of the USCT. On June 15, a force that included the Sixth and Twenty-second USCI attacked and drove back a Confederate skirmish line of infantry strengthened by artillery; it pushed on to capture the outer works, including Batteries Nos. 7–11, a series of formidable redoubts. Two Gettysburg men suffered painful wounds: Joseph Craig, shot in the thigh, and David Stevens, shot in the groin. The painter Andre Castaigne would capture the intensity of this charge on canvas. This dramatic painting, *The Charge of the 22nd Negro Regiment*, now hangs in the Museum of the United States Military Academy at West Point. On June 18, reinforced Confederates hurled back renewed Northern attacks with frightful Union losses. Grant now called for siege operations.

The prospect of a long siege did not appeal to Grant, and when the suggestion came to him that some of his soldiers with coal mining backgrounds excavate a mine under the Rebel works, place a massive charge of explosives, and blast a huge gap in the Southern line, he approved the plan over his own skepticism. Although the plan originally called for a division of black soldiers to spearhead the assault, Grant and Meade, with little advanced notice, changed the plan in favor of a white division leading the assault. Because the change came only hours before the explosion, the lead white division was unprepared and did not properly exploit the breach. The Confederates had time to recover and counterattack, trapping the Union soldiers in the crater created by the explosion. At this point, the assault had clearly failed, but the black troops originally designated to lead the assault were thrown into the hopeless assault. The Forty-third USCT was the only Camp William Penn regiment to participate in the infamous Battle of the Crater. This fight is known to many because it served as an opening scene in the novel and motion picture *Cold Mountain*. The flag of the Forty-third was cut to pieces by withering fire. The men engaged in vicious hand-to-hand fighting but were forced to withdraw. Their brigade commander wrote, "The Forty-third regiment, United States Colored troops, charged over the crest of the crater, and right upon the enemy's works, carrying them, capturing a number of prisoners, a rebel battle-flag, and re-capturing a stand of National colors."

Keeping the pressure on the Confederates, General Grant used his superior numbers to strike simultaneously at different points of the Southern defenses. These coordinated attacks would prevent the defenders from shifting their limited troops to strengthen their line at any one point of attack. Grant's plans in late September called for attacks on three different points of the Richmond defenses: Fort Gilmer, Fort Harrison, and New Market Heights. On September 29, 1864, two Camp William Penn units, the Sixth and Twenty-second USCI, joined many other black regiments in the Battle of New Market Heights, also known as the Battle of Chaffin's Farm. They suffered frightful casualties in a frontal assault on well-entrenched defenders. Sgt. Greenberry Stanton was wounded in the right arm. One company of the Sixth USCI went into battle with thirty-three soldiers; only three emerged from the struggle unharmed. Fourteen African Americans became the recipients of the Medal of Honor on this battlefield, more than on any other battlefield before or since. Most of these medals recognized heroism shown by rescuing a fallen flag or by taking command of a company under fire after all of the white officers had fallen.

After that battle, the Sixth USCI supported the January 15, 1865, assault on Fort Fisher, North Carolina, by fighting back a determined attack of Confederate reinforcements attempting to break through the Union line from the rear. On February 11, the Sixth pushed forward and drove defenders out of Sugar Loaf Hill, North Carolina. Finally, on February 22, they marched into Wilmington, North Carolina, shutting down that heretofore busy center of blockade running.[4]

The battle that inflicted the most grief on Gettysburg's black community was the Battle of Olustee (Ocean Pond) in Florida on February 20, 1864. In this battle, the Eighth USCI, which included seven Gettysburg men, fought desperately against superior Confederate forces. The Confederates took the Union force by surprise. To get into position, the men of the Eighth Regiment ran for half a mile carrying their knapsacks and unloaded rifle muskets, then formed into a line of battle under a devastating fire. One of their white officers, Lt. Oliver W. Norton, a veteran of the fighting at Little Round Top, called it "the most destructive fire I have ever known." During the fight, a bullet ripped through Jonathan Buckmaster's side. George Pennington and Isaac Buckmaster also went down with wounds, all three taken away to the hospital. For Fleming Devan, however, the war had come to a tragic end. Fleming's mother, Sophia Devan, would soon receive a letter from Lieutenant Norton. Since Mrs. Devan could not read, someone had to read to her:

Jacksonville, Florida
   March 10, 1864
   Mrs. Devan:
   Madam:
   I recd. a letter today addressed to Fleming Devan and took the liberty of opening it to learn the address of the writer. It becomes my painful duty to inform you of the death of your son in the Battle of Olustee Fla. Feb. 20, 1864. Flemming was a pet of mine and though from his extreme youth and small stature he seemed poorly fitted for a soldier's life yet he met the enemy like a man and fell bravely fighting_____
   His effects, clothing &c. were all lost in the battle as we were obliged to retreat and leave our dead on the field. He had never been paid and his pay and bounty can now be collected by his nearest relative_____
   Hoping you may receive consolation from a higher source than me, and assuring you of my sympathy in your bereavement I remain.
   Your Obdt. Servant,
   O.W. Norton
   Lieut. Co. "K" 8th U.S.C.T.
   Hilton Head S.C.[5]

There was little time to mourn. Union forces kept up the pressure on Richmond and Petersburg. During the climactic fighting around Petersburg, Rebel fire struck down two black noncommissioned officers from Gettysburg, Sgt. John W. Stanton and Cpl. Samuel L. Mathews. Stanton suffered a bullet wound in the side, while Mathews was shot in the head. Eventually, the Confederate line broke, and Federal troops marched into the two cities.

Jacksonville, Florida,
March 10. 1864,

Mrs. Devan;
     Madam:
              I recd, a letter
today addressed to Fleming
Devan and took the liberty of
opening it to learn the address of the writer. It becomes
my painful duty to inform
you of the death of your son
in the battle of Olustee Fla.
Feb. 20. 1864. Fleming was a
pet of mine and though
from his extreme youth and
small stature he seemed poorly fitted for a soldiers life yet
he met the enemy like a man
and fell bravely fighting——

A letter to Sophia Devan from Oliver W. Norton informing her of the death of her son
Flemming. Courtesy of Arleen Thompson.

His effects, clothing &c. were all lost in the battle as we were obliged to retreat and leave our dead on the field. He had never been paid and his pay and bounty can now be collected by his nearest relative —

Hoping you may receive consolation from a higher source than me, and assuring you of my sympathy in your bereavement I remain.

Your obdt. Servant,
O. W. Norton
Lieut. Co. "K" 8th U.S.C.I.
Hilton Head S. C.

Devan letter (page 2)

Among the first troops to enter both cities were black infantry and cavalry units. The Eighth and Forty-first USCI marched into Petersburg among the first arrivals, while Alonzo Draper's Brigade, including the Twenty-second USCI, had a similar honor at Richmond.

Part of Grant's force, including seven black regiments, pursued the remnants of Robert E. Lee's Army of Northern Virginia and caught up with them at Appomattox Court House. Nearly surrounded, the Rebels made one final attempt to break out of the trap. They attacked the Union lines and forced back the Federal Cavalry. William Birney's USCT, having marched more than ninety miles in three days, reached the field, took position, and stood their ground, and the Southerners fell back. That afternoon in Wilmer McLean's parlor, Lee surrendered his army to General Grant. Three of the seven African American regiments present for the surrender, the Eighth, Forty-first, and 127th, included at least one man from Gettysburg.[6]

But even the end of the war did not bring an end to the work of the African American soldiers. Many were sent to garrison duty throughout the South. Although the bullets stopped flying, death still stalked the ranks of the USCT. In any case, twice as many men died in the American Civil War from disease as from battlefield wounds. John T. Redding of Gettysburg, only a minor when he enlisted, took sick while still in training camp. John's mother, Mary, traveled to Camp William Penn to nurse her youngest son; he was discharged to the care of his mother, but a year later he succumbed to his illness. Three Gettysburg soldiers in the Twenty-fifth USCI—Nelson Royer, Alexander Scott, and John E. Hopkins—came down with severe illness while serving occupation duty in the South. While no Gettysburg men numbered among the 150 or so in their regiment who died, at least two would long feel the residual effects of their wartime illness.

The Eighth USCI, which had suffered such great casualties at Olustee, continued to take losses. William Devan's health broke down on a march to Brownsville, Texas. The hospital staff could not save him. On August 28, 1865, more than four months after Appomattox, Devan passed away. John Watts suffered a leg injury on another Texas march and became lame. The army discharged Watts and sent him home to Gettysburg. Less than a year later, however, he died of complications from his injury.[7]

The news of Abraham Lincoln's assassination shocked the men of the USCT, as shown in many of the letters that they wrote home. The Twenty-second USCI was alerted to join in the search for Lincoln's assassin, but first the regiment was summoned to Washington for a special duty. Thousands of mourners turned out for President Lincoln's funeral on April 19. Two regiments had been detailed to serve as honor guards in the funeral procession from the White House to the Capitol on the afternoon of the nineteenth and from the Capitol to the B&O Station on the twenty-first; the Twenty-second Regiment, because of its reputation for a good soldierly appearance, was one of them, receiving the assignment of escorting its fallen commander-in-chief. At one point, the Twenty-second USCI led the entire funeral procession.[8]

Notes

1. Harry Bradshaw Matthews, *Whence They Came: Families of United States Col·ored Troops in Gettysburg, Pennsylvania, 1815–1871* (privately published, 1992), 44, 47; Harry Bradshaw Matthews, *Revisiting the Battle of Gettysburg: The Presence of African Americans before and after the Conflict* (Oneonta, NY: privately published, 1995), 7–9; Betty Dorsey Myers, *Segregation in Death: Gettysburg's Lincoln Cemetery* (Gettysburg, PA: Lincoln Cemetery Project Association, 2001), 64–75; Samuel P. Bates, *History of Pennsylvania Volunteers, 1861–5*, 5 vols. (Harrisburg, PA: B. Singerly, State Printer, 1869–1871). Volume 5 contains rosters of black regiments raised in Pennsylvania.

2. Dudley T. Cornish, *The Sable Arm: Negro Troops in the Union Army* (New York: Longmans Green, 1956; Lawrence: University Press of Kansas, 1987); Noah Andre Trudeau, *Like Men of War: Black Troops in the Civil War, 1862–1865* (Boston: Little, Brown, 1998); William A. Gladstone, *Men of Color* (Gettysburg, PA: Thomas, 1993).

3. Matthews, *Whence They Came*, 20; Matthews, *Revisiting the Battle of Gettysburg*, 8.

4. Matthews, *Revisiting the Battle of Gettysburg*, 7–9; Trudeau, *Like Men of War*, 220–27, 284–93, 314–31, 358–62; Paradis, 48–60, 69–79, 81–86.

5. Trudeau, *Like Men of War*, 137–51; Matthews, *Revisiting the Battle of Gettysburg*, 7; letter, O. W. Norton to Mrs. [Sophia] Devan, Pension File, Flemming Devan, NA.

6. Matthews, *Revisiting the Battle of Gettysburg*, 9; Trudeau, *Like Men of War*, 418–32.

7. Matthews, *Revisiting the Battle of Gettysburg*, 7–9.

8. Trudeau, *Like Men of War*, 433–34; Gladstone, *Men of Color*, 67.

CHAPTER SIX

~

Little Note nor Long Remember

Lincoln Cemetery

For many years before the Civil War, Gettysburg's black cemetery stood on the east side of town, at Fourth Street near York Street. By the end of 1864, the town's African American community had concluded that it would need a new cemetery, particularly for the eventual burial of the many local black Civil War veterans. Members of St. Paul's AME Zion Church formed the Sons of Good Will in December 1864. They declared as their goal the establishment of a new black cemetery. In particular, they aimed to provide a final resting place that would fittingly honor African American war veterans.

Land for the new cemetery came from Edan Devan, perhaps the wealthiest black resident of the borough. People whispered that Devan had come by much of this money by dishonorable means. Rumors abounded that he had informed on fugitive slaves to Southern slave hunters and had earned bounties for his betrayals. Regardless of Devan's alleged treachery, no one can deny that the Devan family paid a high price in the fight for liberty. Four local Devans marched off with the USCT. Edan's son, William H. Devan, a musician in Company A of the Eighth USCI, died at Brownsville, Texas, on August 28, 1865. Robert Wesley Devan of Company B of the Forty-third USCI died in a military hospital in Portsmouth, Virginia, on February 24, 1865. Fleming Devan of the Eighth USCI was killed in action at Olustee, Florida, on February 20, 1864. Only Solomon Devan of Company F of the Twenty-second USCI survived the war.

Gettysburg's African American burial ground took the name "Lincoln Cemetery." Eventually, some thirty black veterans of the American Civil War would be laid to rest there.

The Sons of Good Will also gave some financial support to at least five black Civil War veterans. Of the five elected officers of the organization, all but the treasurer, Basil Biggs, were veterans themselves. One of the founding members of the organization, Lloyd F. Watts, had become one of the most respected citizens of the town. Watts, like many other Gettysburg residents, was born in the slave state of Maryland. His family moved to Pennsylvania, where Watts worked to support his widowed mother and six siblings. An ordained deacon of St. Paul's AME Zion Church, he served for years as president of its Board of Trustees. He also served for years as the principal instructor at Gettysburg's "Colored School."[1]

The Battle of Gettysburg continued to inflict injury and grief long after the fight was over. On March 1, 1864, the *Adams Sentinel* reported a "distressing accident" that had taken place on Monday, February 22:

> Several boys, aged about 15 years, were amusing themselves with a gun from the battlefield (shooting mark, we believe) when the contents of the discharges entered the head of a little colored girl, who was near the spot, inflicting a mortal wound in the head. She died on Wednesday, aged about seven years.[2]

Other consequences continued long after the war. John Watts never recovered from his wartime disability; it contributed to his death in 1866. Sophia Devan continued to grieve over the loss of her son Flemming. Lydia Devan Watts happily welcomed her husband, John, home from the war, but he stunned her with the news that her cherished brother William would never come home. The siblings had been so close that they had chosen to have a double wedding ceremony. William had married Mary Walker, who bore them a child, Henrietta. William had had only two years to delight in his daughter before marching off to war. Now Mary Walker Devan would have to raise Henrietta alone. In 1866, John Watts died from complications of the leg ailment that he contracted during his military service. A variety of illnesses contracted during his service time left John Hopkins to be discharged blind in one eye and nearly blind in the other.[3]

The town's black community never recovered from the trauma of the war. Many citizens who fled from the Rebel invasion did not come back to Gettysburg. Those who owned no real property were especially unlikely to return. The 1870 census showed more black residents in town than the 1860 census had, but the names had changed extensively. Less than half of

GETTYSBURG, PENNSYLVANIA

I received my check on Wed. Nov. 1
opend it and thought I laid it
some where in my room. we had looked
the house over. but cannot find it.
My pension is the only income that I
have to live on. and I am old and
unable to work. I am the only colord
civial war widow in this town and
as near as I can come to my age I am
well up in 80. having been a slave
and sold on the block when quite a
girl in Va. so if their is anything Sir that
you can do to help me God knows that
I will appreciate it. my serial no. is.
744.956 name Mrs Harriet C. Stanton
Widow of Samuel M. Stanton.
145 W. Breckenridge St.
Gettysburg Pa
Thank you for your
kindness.

Letter from Harriet Stanton, widow of Samuel Stanton, Company C, Third U.S. Colored
Infantry. She never knew her age because she had been so young when she was sold on
the auction block. Courtesy of Pension Records, National Archives.

the 186 African Americans in the 1860 census numbered among the 239 in 1870. Newly freed men and women from Maryland and other Southern states moved into boroughs. One attraction for the new neighbors was the new jobs connected with the growing tourist trade. Just as before the war, the most common occupation for a black resident of Gettysburg was "day laborer," but the number of blacks working in hotels more than doubled. This trend reflected the growing tourist industry of the town.

Abraham Brien sold his farm in 1869 at a considerable profit. This allowed him to move into the town, where he lived in comfortable semiretirement until he died in 1879. Basil Biggs moved into the Fisher farmhouse on Cemetery Ridge when he inherited the property in John Fisher's will in 1863. Biggs later purchased the adjoining property of Peter Frey and lived there until 1894, when he purchased a home on the corner of Washington and High Streets. His harmonious marriage to Mary lasted over sixty years. He died in his eighty-seventh year, his obituary remembering him as a "highly respected" citizen.

Owen Robinson faced some unfortunate experiences. When he fled town in 1863, he entrusted his two valuable hogs to a neighbor for concealment. The noisy hogs, however, gave away their hiding place to some hungry soldiers. Robinson served for years after the battle as sexton of the Presbyterian Church. The church had been used as a hospital, and many of the wounded had died in that building. This convinced the sexton that the church was haunted. Youngsters in the town delighted in exploiting his fears, playing impish pranks to simulate a haunting.

John Hopkins continued his employment as janitor at Pennsylvania College. The students loved him. One yearbook playfully identified Hopkins as "Vice-President" of the college. Only twice has it been recorded that the entire school turned out en masse for an event—once to hear Lincoln give his Gettysburg Address and once to attend the funeral of John Hopkins.[4]

The earlier-mentioned Lydia Smith, the poor black woman who brought aid to wounded soldiers of both sides, should not be confused with better-known Lydia Hamilton Smith. The latter Smith, born in Gettysburg in 1815, was married and had two children before being widowed in 1852. She became the housekeeper of U.S. congressman Thaddeus Stevens, whom she had known when he had lived in Gettysburg. Stevens had moved his law practice from Gettysburg to Lancaster and offered Smith the position. While in Lancaster, Smith not only performed the duties of a housekeeper but also managed Stevens's finances and became his confidante. The abolitionist Stevens assisted freedom seekers from the South and paid local residents to keep an eye on known slave catchers operating in the vicinity. Smith is believed to have been part of these Underground Railroad activities. Evidence supporting this conclusion includes a large cistern located near Lydia Hamilton Smith's home on Stevens's property. Archaeologists who have examined the cistern indicate that it may have been used to conceal people. Tradition holds that escapees from slavery who reached Wrightsville would be concealed on a train that would take them to Lancaster and their next stop—the homes of Stevens and Smith.

While the Lydia Smith in the story was a "poor woman," Lydia Hamilton Smith defiantly was not. By the time of the Battle of Gettysburg, she owned multiple properties and was becoming an exceptional businesswoman. Lydia's son Isaac joined the Sixth USCI a short time after the Gettysburg Campaign.

On January 25, 1869, Frederick Douglass visited Gettysburg to lecture. In his speech at Agricultural Hall, he praised the conduct of black soldiers in the late war and their part in securing the victory. He emphasized the importance of ratifying the proposed Fifteenth Amendment to the Constitution, guaranteeing the right to vote regardless of race. Douglass urged that blacks exercise their right to vote and hold public office. The Republican *Star and Sentinel* strongly supported equal rights, while the opposition's newspaper *The Compiler* thoroughly ridiculed that idea. A large-enough segment of the white community agreed with *The Compiler* to jeopardize both equal rights and the memory of black contributions in the war.[5]

The first disturbing sign for the future came on Memorial Day of 1869, Sunday, May 30. The public ceremony for the day reflected the increasing attitude of reconciliation between the Blue and the Grey. The ceremony would honor the dead of both sides alike. As originally planned, children from the local Sabbath schools would take part in the procession and place flowers on the graves of the soldiers.

A few of the white participants objected to the inclusion of the colored Sabbath school in the ceremony. Enough objections arose that the black children were excluded from the procession. *The Compiler* enthusiastically supported the decision to exclude blacks and took the occasion afterward to point out that on the day of the ceremony, a black alderman shared a carriage ride with the mayor of Washington, DC, while wounded white soldiers hobbled along on foot. The paper went on to warn of similar outrages to come should the Fifteenth Amendment be passed. The *Star and Sentinel*, however, blasted the decision, pointing out that the brave Union dead honored by the ceremony "did not deem it unworthy of their manhood to stand side by side with the colored soldiers of the Republic, amid the crash of shot and shell."[6]

Black veterans kept alive the memories of their contributions by forming their own Grand Army of the Republic posts. In Chambersburg, the Maj. Martin Delaney Post, formed in 1885, continued until 1893 and included twenty-four members at one point. In Carlisle, the Jesse G. Thompson Post (1884–1920) reached thirty-five members at its zenith. As years passed, the exclusion of blacks from memorial ceremonies became institutionalized. The planners of the 1913 Gettysburg reunion of Civil War veterans did not invite surviving black veterans, and as African American veterans passed away, the memory of their contributions to the Union victory also seemed to pass away.

The irony of these "Jim Crow" reunions was not lost on black leaders. The same reunion that excluded veterans of the USCT who had fought to preserve the Union and destroy slavery welcomed the Confederate veterans who had "fought to destroy the Union and perpetuate slavery" and now continued to reject attempts to establish basic civil rights. Frederick Douglass pointed out that in the name of reconciling whites North and South, the nation seemed willing to "remember with equal admiration those who struck at the nation's life, and those who struck to save it—those who fought for slavery and those who fought for liberty and justice." Douglass feared, "If war among the whites brought peace and liberty to the blacks, what will peace among the whites bring?"[7]

Today

Much of Gettysburg National Military Park is as attractive as it is because of the labor of African Americans. Nineteenth-century photographs show black workers landscaping and building the roads that became the park that visitors see today. Lloyd Watts, then in his late fifties, worked erecting monuments until chest and joint pain disabled him.[8]

Half a century later, during the Great Depression, black laborers from a Civilian Conservation Corps camp worked to improve the roads and drainage systems and erect markers that tourists now take for granted. Until recently, none of these thousands of markers indicated the involvement of African Americans in this conflict. The few such markers found at Gettysburg today still fail to provide adequate historical interpretation of African American participation in the conflict. Thus, few blacks today feel any connection with this historic site. Many visit with school groups on field trips, but of all the visitors who come to the park on their own, barely one in a hundred is an African American.

Eventually, some African Americans stepped forward to claim their due. Photographs of later reunions of Civil War veterans, such as the seventy-fifth anniversary reunion at Gettysburg, show a few black veterans, some wearing metals.

Any pilgrimage to Gettysburg must include a visit to the National Cemetery, where simple stone markers honor men for their sacrifices. Most of the men buried in the Civil War section were killed at Gettysburg, but some died later in the war or after it. Few visitors note that two of the headstones bear inscriptions identifying them as the final resting places of veterans of the USCT. One of the graves belongs to Charles H. Parker, whose body reached this site through a roundabout route. Parker was originally buried at the African American church at Yellow Hill, north of Gettysburg. Over the years, the church was destroyed and abandoned and its graveyard neglected and overgrown. Tombstones were broken or disappeared entirely. During the Great Depression, the federal government funded a program that sought out the gravesites of veterans to ensure burials with dignity. At Yellow Hill, investigators found two USCT gravesites, those of William H. Mathews and Charles H. Parker. They reinterred Matthews's remains at Lincoln Cemetery but removed Parker's body to the Gettysburg National Cemetery. Parker served in the Eighth USCI. He was wounded at Gainesville and developed pneumonia as a result. He was discharged but suffered a chronic cough that continued until his death.

The other headstone is that of Henry Gooden, who served with the 127th USCT. This unit numbered·among the seven black regiments that pursued the retreating army of Robert E. Lee all the way to Appomattox Court House. Gooden's presence at the National Cemetery, near the site of Lincoln's address, symbolizes the role of African Americans in this great conflict. Two great armies fought at Gettysburg, the best army on each side. Yet, the 180,000 or more African Americans who served in the uniform of the U.S. Army during the war exceeded in number the combined blue and grey forces that fought at Gettysburg. The thousands of white soldiers who struggled and died on the Gettysburg battlefield had nobly advanced the cause, but those fallen heroes could no longer carry on the fight. They passed much of that duty on to the black volunteers, who with equal nobility would carry on the fight until victory was won. The world, however, would little note nor long remember what they did. Perhaps now their story will be told.[9]

Notes

1. Betty Dorsey Myers, *Segregation in Death: Gettysburg's Lincoln Cemetery* (Gettysburg, PA: Lincoln Cemetery Project Association, 2001), 7–8, 64–75; G. Craig Caba, ed., *Episodes of Gettysburg and the Underground Railroad: As Witnessed and Recorded by*

Professor J. Howard Wert (Gettysburg, PA: privately published, 1998), 59; Peter C. Vermilyea, "The Effect of the Confederate Invasion of Pennsylvania on Gettysburg's African American Community," *The Gettysburg Magazine* 24 (January 2001), 124; Harry Bradshaw Matthews, *Whence They Came: Families of United States Colored Troops in Gettysburg, Pennsylvania, 1815–1871* (privately published, 1992), 19, 25, 108; Harry Bradshaw Matthews, *Revisiting the Battle of Gettysburg: The Presence of African Americans before and after the Conflict* (Oneonta, NY: privately published, 1995), 12; Margaret S. Creighton, *The Colors of Courage: Gettysburg's Hidden History: Immigrants, Women, and African-Americans in the Civil War's Defining Battle* (New York: Basic, 2005), 62–63.

2. *The Adams Sentinel*, March 1, 1864, in William A. Frassanito, *Early Photography at Gettysburg* (Gettysburg, PA: Thomas, 1995).

3. Matthews, *Revisiting the Battle of Gettysburg*, 10–11, 16; Vermilyea, "The Effect of the Confederate Invasion," 124–25.

4. Vermilyea, "The Effect of the Confederate Invasion," 125; African American Civilian Files, Abraham Bryan, Basil Biggs, Owen Robinson; Charles M. McCurdy, *Gettysburg: A Memoir* (Pittsburgh, PA: Reed & Witting, 1929), 6.

5. Matthews, *Revisiting the Battle of Gettysburg*, 14; *The Compiler*, January 29, 1869; historical marker at intersection of High and West streets, Gettysburg, PA.

6. Matthews, *Revisiting the Battle of Gettysburg*, 14–15, 28n; "Our Dead Heroes," *The Star and Sentinel*, May 21, June 4, June 11, 1869; "Dedication of the Monument," *The Gettysburg Compiler*, July 9, 1869.

7. David W. Blight, *Race and Reunion: The Civil War in American Memory* (Cambridge, MA: Harvard University Press, 2001), 9–11, 106, 132.

8. Creighton, *The Colors of Courage*, 222–23.

9. Debra Sandoe McCauslin, "Black Civil War Veterans from Biglerville," ACHS; Individual Service Records, Charles Gooden, William H. Matthews, Charles H. Parker, National Archives; RG 79, T and TM, Still Pictures Branch, National Archives. For a list of black veterans known to have attended the commemoration of the seventy-fifth anniversary of the Battle of Gettysburg, see Appendix B. For a map indicating burial sites of the two USCT veterans buried in the Soldiers' National Cemetery, see Appendix C.

~

Appendix A:
Letter of Frederic Capron

Smithfield, (Near Lonsdale, R.I.)
March 15th, 1867

My Dear Parents,

From this far off country and continent I write to you, that you may know that I am still alive and remember; and often think of you, and of all my brothers and sisters, and of our Island home [Zanzibar]. You have no doubt often wondered what became of me, and perhaps have given me up as lost to you forever. (For I never believed the story of those men who took me away, that you sent them to take me away with them.) I will tell you how it was so far as I know.—It was in the year of 1861, now six years ago, I had gone out from you towards night and was playing with 5 or 6 other boys on the beach when five men from a ship came up, took me in their arms, in spite of all my kicks and screams & forced me into a boat and on board their ship. I tried all I could to get from them, but could not. The ship was the Sea Ranger, Capt. Green belonging to the port of Boston, Massachusetts, U.S.A. The names of the men who seized me on the shore were, Henry Spaulding—Cook—and Collins, I don't remember the others. We had a great storm at sea during the passage, and I was very sea-sick. The men were very good to me, and some said my father had sent me to America to learn something. I did not believe them. We arrived in Boston, Mass. in May, and Mr. Spaulding took me the following day with him to Woonsocket, a town in the state of Rhode Island, which is one of the New England and North states where they have not held our people as slaves for a long time. I am still living in this state in the town of Smithfield adjoining that of Woonsocket, with a gentleman, Mr. Christopher C. Dexter, a farmer, and who is very kind to me. He tells me to get a good education, and learn to do things and be somebody worth while then I may be an engineer or may be a ship's captain, and then come home perhaps. I want to come home, I often want to come right away. There was a great war in this country of which you must have heard, it lasted four years. Mr. Dexter's nephew is an officer in the army—Captain Walcott—I went to the war with him in 1863, to attend him, we were in the great battle of Gettysburg, and my master lost a leg in that battle, I nursed him till the surgeons took him away, and afterwards returned to Mr. Dexter's. I work and go to school. I learn reading and writing, and some geography and arithmetic. I have a beautiful teacher, a young lady who is very kind to me, and has given me some assistance to write this to you, my dear father and mother, that you may know that I am living and where I am, and how glad I would be to see and come to you again. When this reaches you please to write to me. It should be directed—

Lonsdale R. Island,
United States of America.

Yours Affectionately,
Frederic Capron

Courtesy of Gettysburg National Military Park Archives, Gladstone Collection.

~

Appendix B: Black Veterans at the Seventy-fifth Anniversary Reunion at Gettysburg

Black veterans who attended the 1938 reunion at Gettysburg, with their age in 1938 and unit, if known.

Francis M. Brown, Kansas City, Kansas, age 95, Company A, Eleventh U.S. Colored Troops

C. T. Budd, Birmingham, Alabama, age and unit unknown

John C. Cook, Oklahoma City, Oklahoma, age 100, Company A, Seventh U.S. Colored Troops

Reed Crider, Metropolis, Illinois, age 94, Company F, Eighth U.S. Colored Heavy Artillery

Albert E. Eggleston, Tuscumbia, Alabama, age 94, Company A, Fifty-fifth U.S. Colored Troops

Benjamin Franklin, Alcoa, Tennessee, age 94, precise unit unknown

Charlie Garrett, Clarksville, Tennessee, age 92, precise unit unknown

Joshua Green, Maysville, Kentucky, age 91, Company G, Thirteenth U.S. Colored Heavy Artillery

David Harper, Montgomery, Missouri, age 90, precise unit unknown

Fred Harris, Helena, Alaska, age 95, precise unit unknown

William Henderson, Hamilton County, Tennessee, age 98, precise unit unknown

Peter R. Hogan, Parsons, Kansas, age 95, Company 1, Twenty-seventh U.S. Colored Troops

Richard Holmes, Rockport, IN, age 90, precise unit unknown

George W. Johnson, Kansas City, Missouri, age 89, precise unit unknown

Spencer Jones, Caroline County, Maryland, age 91, precise unit unknown

David Moody, Dayton, Ohio, age 100, precise unit unknown

David Penny, Beaver Falls, Pennsylvania, age 93, Company H, Fifth U.S. Colored Troops

John B. Reynolds, Zanesville, Ohio, age 90, precise unit unknown

James Riley, Chandler, Oklahoma, age 93, Company B, Eighty-first U.S. Colored Troops

George Roberts, Tensas County, Louisiana, age 89, precise unit known

John Roberts, Slough, Alabama, age 95, precise unit unknown

Peter R. Robinson, Dent, Alaska, age 95, Company B, Thirty-fourth U.S. Colored Troops

William Sebastian, East Donagal, Pennsylvania, age 93, Company B, One hundred sixteenth U.S. Colored Troops

Alvin Smith, Perkins, Ohio, age 93, Company H, Twenty-seventh U.S. Colored Troops

Richard M. Smith, Beaufort, South Carolina, age 94, precise unit unknown

Emory Steward, Indian Valley, Idaho, age unknown, Company I, Thirty-ninth U.S. Colored Troops

George W. Still, Brooklyn, New York, age 90, Company E, Twenty-sixth U.S. Colored Troops

Josiah Waddle, Omaha, Nebraska, age 96, Company H, Seventh-eighth U.S. Colored Troops

Thomas Walters, Los Angeles, California, age 92, Fifth Mass. Colored Calvary

John W. Wamble, Boynton, Oklahoma, age 85, Company B, One hundred thirty-seventh U.S. Colored Troops

George Williams, Boston, Georgia, age 92, precise unit unknown

James Willis, East Orange, New Jersey, age 100, Battery A, Second U.S. Colored Light Artillery, and Company C, One hundred twenty-seventh U.S. Colored Troops

John A. Wilson, Fawn, Pennsylvania, age 91, precise unit unknown

Mack Wilson, Greenville, Mississippi, age 92, precise unit unknown

Richard Wilson, St. Francisville, Louisiana, age 93, Company L, Sixth U.S. Colored Heavy Artillery and Company C, Fifty-eighth U.S. Colored Troops

Note: Addresses of the veterans are according to the 1930 U.S. Census.
Courtesy of Gettysburg National Military Park, research by Paul Shevchuk.

~

Appendix C: Gettysburg and African Americans— A Tour for Today

The Visitor Center occupies the area between Taneytown Road and Baltimore Pike with exits to each street. Exit the Visitor Center by way of Taneytown Road and turn right onto Taneytown Road. In about 0.3 miles, you will go up a hill, where the National Cemetery rests on the right. Set your trip odometer to 0.0 as you pass the gates to the National Cemetery on your right.

Continue driving north and cross Von Steinwer. The road now becomes South Washington. You are now driving through what was the town's black neighborhood in 1863, the southwest corner of town. The tour begins and ends here. You may want to park and take a walking tour using the more detailed map "Black Residents and Points of Interest" (Appendix D), or you may continue driving and save the walking tour for the end of the driving tour. On the right when you reach Breckinridge Street, you will see St. Paul's African Methodist Episcopal Zion Church, built fifty-four years after the battle. This is the third location of the African Methodist Episcopal church. During the Civil War, two black residences occupied this property. Singleton Weldon owned a two-story house on the southern half of the present-day church property, and Ann Chiller shared the house with him. Upton Johnson owned a one-story frame house on the northern half of the property. His son Randolph led a militia of black men from Gettysburg. On the right at 219 South Washington stands the house owned by John Hopkins. At the time of the battle, Hopkins did not live here; he and his wife lived on the campus of Pennsylvania (Gettysburg) College because of his employment as the school janitor.

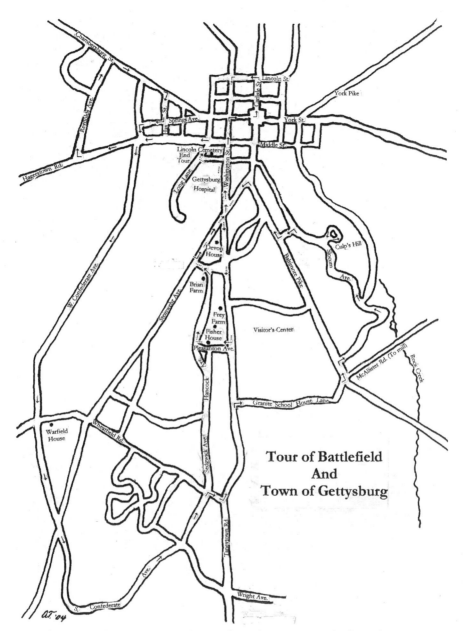

Gettysburg and African Americans: A tour for today. Courtesy of Arleen Thompson.

At 0.9 miles, turn right onto Chambersburg. After making the turn, you will see on the left the location of the law office of white abolitionist Thaddeus Stevens; on the right stands Christ Lutheran Church, the reported hiding place for local blacks to avoid capture by Confederates.

You will come to a circle—travel three-quarters of the way around the circle and turn north onto Carlisle. Halfway around the circle you will see a gray building, the Wills House, where President Lincoln stayed when he came here to deliver his Gettysburg Address. One block up Carlisle, you will see a train station on the right. Lincoln's train arrived here. He may have been met by a porter such as Margaret Palm, who earned money carrying travelers' bags and trunks at this station.

Continue to the traffic light and go 1.4 miles, and turn left onto Lincoln. This is the campus of Gettysburg College; it was called Pennsylvania College at the time of the battle. Turn left at the first stop sign, the 1.5-mile marker. An unofficial fraternity at the college, the Black Ducks, risked imprisonment by aiding fugitive slaves in their escape. John Hopkins lived on campus with his wife in a house that stood near the present location of Musselman Library. The Hopkinses reported the loss of hundreds of dollars' worth of property taken or destroyed during the battle.

Daniel Alexander Payne, a black student at the nearby Lutheran Theological Seminary, taught classes to black residents of the town in a classroom provided by the college. A historical marker stands near the Civil War Institute at 300 North Washington Street. The marker commemorates Reverend Payne, who went on to become a bishop in the African Methodist Episcopal church. The traffic light ahead marks the intersection of Washington and Chambersburg; at the northeast corner of the intersection, a historical marker points out the site of the Eagle Hotel. Samuel Stanton lived here, where he tended the stables until he enlisted in the Third Regiment of the U.S. Colored Infantry. He returned after his discharge and worked here for several more years until he was kicked by a horse and crippled for life.

Cross Chambersburg; at 2.0 miles, turn right onto Middle Street. Drive for 1.0 mile on Middle Street and turn right at 3.0 onto Reynolds Avenue. On the first day of the battle, the commander of the First Corps of the Union's Army of the Potomac, John Reynolds, held back the Confederates, who pushed forward from your left. A Confederate bullet struck down Reynolds as he directed his troops. He was the highest-ranking general killed in the battle on either side. On your right, you will pass a statue of General Abner Doubleday, who took over the command of the First Corps after Reynolds fell. Doubleday was at one time credited with inventing the game of baseball.

Whether this is true or not, the Baseball Hall of Fame stands in Doubleday's hometown, Cooperstown, New York.

Beyond the statue in front of the trees on the left, you will see a mound of earth. The marker on this mound indicates the spot where John Reynolds was killed. At the traffic light at 3.7 miles, turn right onto Route 30, Chambersburg Pike. At 4.1, turn right onto Hay Street. To your right, you will see the Lutheran Theological Seminary. This is the seminary where Reverend Payne studied. The green-domed cupola was used as an observation post at different times by Union generals Buford and Reynolds and by Confederate general Robert E. Lee.

Turn right onto Springs Avenue, then turn left at the stop sign at 4.4 miles. Cross over Middle Street, and continue driving straight along Confederate Avenue. This road did not exist at the time of the battle. It runs along the line held by the Confederates on the last two days of the battle. After driving about a half mile, you will see on your left the North Carolina memorial, a dramatic group statue of Confederates soldiers advancing with their flag. This statue was created by Gutzon Borglum, the same artist who designed the presidential images on Mount Rushmore and the original plans for the carvings of Confederate leaders at Stone Mountain, Georgia.

From this point on, as you look to your left, you will be looking across the famous field of "Pickett's Charge." Further ahead on your left, you will observe the Virginia Memorial, crowned with a mounted statue of Robert E. Lee, the commander of the Confederate Army of Northern Virginia. Somewhere near this point, the general observed his ill-fated assault.

Continue on to the stop sign at 6.5 miles. On your left near this intersection, on the opposite side of the street, stands a home with three garages. The original part of this home, the stone section, was the home of an African American blacksmith. On the second day of the battle, Confederate troops advanced through his property and attacked the Union lines to the east. General James Longstreet, the Confederate second in command, pitched his tent near here and may have used the Warfield house for a time as his headquarters. When Warfield returned to his home after the battle, he found extensive damage to all of his buildings, gardens, and orchards. He lost all of his livestock, wheat, corn, and blacksmithing equipment, and he found fourteen Confederate graves in his garden.

Cross over Middletown Road. The cannon barrel embedded in the ground on the right marks the spot where General Longstreet pitched his tent and established his headquarters. Continue to the stop sign at 7.2 miles. Carefully cross the highway and continue straight on the tour route. At the 8.7-mile point, you will continue up the hill to the top of Little Round Top. The armies fought desperately for control of this hill on the second day of the battle. You may want to park your car and climb to the top of the hill for an impressive view of the battlefield. When you return to your car, continue on to the stop sign at 9.1 miles, and turn right onto Sykes Avenue.

Carefully turn left at mile 9.3 onto Taneytown Road (Route 134). Turn right at mile 10.1 onto Granite Schoolhouse Road. At the stop sign at mile 10.7, you will be near the location of the Union army's reserve artillery and its ammunition wagon train. It would play a crucial role in repelling the Confederates on the second and third days of the battle. Turn left at this stop sign, and continue to the stop sign at 10.9 miles. Across the street, you will see McAllister Road. This is privately owned now, but at the time of the battle, a dirt road ran back into the woods to McAllister Mill, an important station on the Underground Railroad.

Carefully turn left onto Baltimore Road. At mile 11.1, turn right onto an unmarked park road. After the turn, you will see a sign for Culp's Hill and Spangler's Spring. At the stop sign, follow the auto tour signs to Culp's Hill. Continue following the auto tour sign up the winding road, all the way to the top of Culp's Hill. On your right as you climb the hill, you may see traces of the defensive trenches dug by the Union soldiers who defended this hill. At the top of the hill, stop at the observation tower at 12.4 miles.

You may want to climb the observation tower for a view of the town and this part of the battlefield. About 100 feet northwest of the base of the observation tower, near where the circle of pavement merges into a single road, you may find a split rock or two parallel rocks with a few feet of space between them. The rocks stand about twenty feet from the paved road. Before the Civil War, this spot served as a hiding place for freedom-seeking fugitive slaves. People defying the Fugitive Slave Law fashioned a roof of wood and covered it with dirt and leaves, leaving only a small entrance to the "cave" on the downhill side.

Returning to your car, continue downhill, following the tour route, and turn left where the road splits. At the stop sign at 12.8 miles, turn right onto Baltimore Road. As you drive up Baltimore Road, you will pass cannon emplacements where Union troops repelled a determined Confederate attack late on the second day of fighting. The attacking Confederates included at least one free black man from Louisiana, Charles H. Lutz. The second of two equestrian statues on the hill remembers General Oliver Otis Howard, a religious man who headed the Freedmen's Bureau at the end of the war. Howard oversaw the establishment of schools for African Americans; Howard University is named for him.

At the traffic light at 13.2 miles, make a hard left onto Steinwehr Avenue. At 13.3, turn left onto Taneytown Road (Route 134). After passing the gates to the National Cemetery, you will see a small white house on the right. This is the Leister House, which served as headquarters for Major General George Gordon Meade, commander of the Union forces. Next on the right, you will pass a large barn, part of the Peter Frey farm. After the war, this farm was purchased by Basil Biggs, an African American farmer and veterinarian. At 14.3, turn right onto Pleasanton Avenue, following the tour route. The white farmhouse that you will see as you turn onto Pleasanton is the Hummelbaugh house. Between this house and the Frey barn stood the house of John Fisher, a black farmer who died within months of the Battle of Gettysburg. He left his home to Basil Biggs in his will. Biggs moved into the home and later purchased the adjoining Frey farm.

Continue to the stop sign at 14.6 miles, and turn right. The small grove of trees ahead on the left was the focal point of Pickett's Charge on the third and final day of the battle. The Confederates attacked across the open field to your left and were driven back by the Union defenders, who used the stone wall near the clump of trees for protection. This stone wall was part of the property owned by a prosperous black farmer, Abraham Brien. The Brien (Bryan) farmhouse and barn stand just ahead, on either side of the road. You may want to stop and read the historical marker and view the farmhouse and the barn, still showing its battle scars.

Continue to the stop sign at 15.2 and turn left. At 15.3, turn right onto Steinwehr. At the traffic light at Washington (15.6) turn left. Turn left again onto Gettys Street at 15.8 miles. At Long Lane (16.0), turn right. The last stop of the tour is the Lincoln Cemetery. Buried at the cemetery are James Warfield, Owen Robinson, Abraham Brien, and his first and second wives. Also buried here are some thirty black Civil War veterans. Some of them returned from the war with lifelong disabilities. Other black citizens of Gettysburg did not return, some dying of disease in the service and one, Flemming Devan, killed in action at the Battle of Olustee.

Ten years after the Battle of Gettysburg, at a memorial service held at this cemetery, the speaker, Aaron Russell, addressed the participants:

What can be said of the heroic, self-sacrificing spirit which actuated the colored soldier during the four eventful years of the late Rebellion? . . . For it can be said of the colored soldier, as of none other, that he fought for a country that had not recognized his citizenship. Helping to bear its burdens, and enduring all the responsibilities incident to citizenship, he thus showed to the world that his aspirations and his longings were for a recognition, of his Manhood by the country of his nativity, upon which alone depended the future elevation of his race. What a noble example!

Then let us bedeck these grassy grounds with flowers, as an evidence that the heroism of the colored soldiers is still green in our memories. Yes! We will ever hold them in grateful remembrance.[1]

Note

1. Betty Dorsey Meyers, *Segregation in Death: Gettysburg's Lincoln Cemetery* (Gettysburg, PA: Lincoln Cemetery Project Association, 2001), 89–90, from Gettysburg *Star and Sentinel*, June 4, 1873.

SOLDIERS' NATIONAL CEMETERY

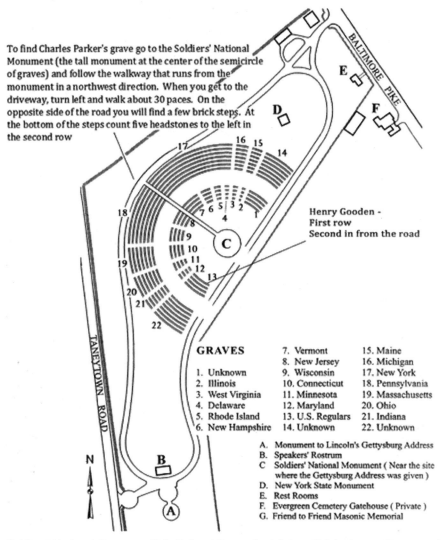

To find Charles Parker's grave go to the Soldiers' National Monument (the tall monument at the center of the semicircle of graves) and follow the walkway that runs from the monument in a northwest direction. When you get to the driveway, turn left and walk about 30 paces. On the opposite side of the road you will find a few brick steps. At the bottom of the steps count five headstones to the left in the second row

Henry Gooden - First row Second in from the road

GRAVES

1. Unknown
2. Illinois
3. West Virginia
4. Delaware
5. Rhode Island
6. New Hampshire
7. Vermont
8. New Jersey
9. Wisconsin
10. Connecticut
11. Minnesota
12. Maryland
13. U.S. Regulars
14. Unknown
15. Maine
16. Michigan
17. New York
18. Pennsylvania
19. Massachusetts
20. Ohio
21. Indiana
22. Unknown

A. Monument to Lincoln's Gettysburg Address
B. Speakers' Rostrum
C Soldiers' National Monument (Near the site where the Gettysburg Address was given)
D. New York State Monument
E. Rest Rooms
F. Evergreen Cemetery Gatehouse (Private)
G. Friend to Friend Masonic Memorial

Soldiers' National Cemetery: U.S. Colored Troops burial sites. Original map. Courtesy of National Parks Service, Gettysburg National Military Park. Modified with permission of the National Parks Service by Jack Newman.

~

Appendix D: Black Residents and Points of Interest in the Town of Gettysburg

Houses in Gettysburg did not have numbered addresses at the time of the battle. Modern-day addresses are used here. Where the original building site is now vacant or built over, *italics* are used for the addresses.

1. *North Washington Street* (beyond the map) on the campus of Pennsylvania (Gettysburg) College—John Hopkins, janitor for the college, lived here with his wife, Julia, and their son, John Edward, who enlisted in the Twenty-fifth U.S. Colored Infantry.
2. *Northeast corner of Washington and Chambersburg streets*—the Eagle Hotel, Samuel Stanton lived here where he worked as a stable hand until he enlisted in the Third Regiment of U.S. Colored Infantry. He returned after his discharge and worked here for several more years until he was kicked by a horse and crippled for life.
3. *219 South Washington Street*—house owned by John Hopkins. Hopkins moved in 1860 from this house to one provided on campus by Pennsylvania College (see historical marker).
4. *220 South Washington Street*—Clara Digges owned a story-and-a-half frame house; another family, Samuel, Elizabeth and Lucy Butler, also lived here.
5. 263 South Washington Street—Upton Johnson owned a one-story frame house on the northern half of the present-day property of St. Paul African Methodist Episcopal Zion Church.

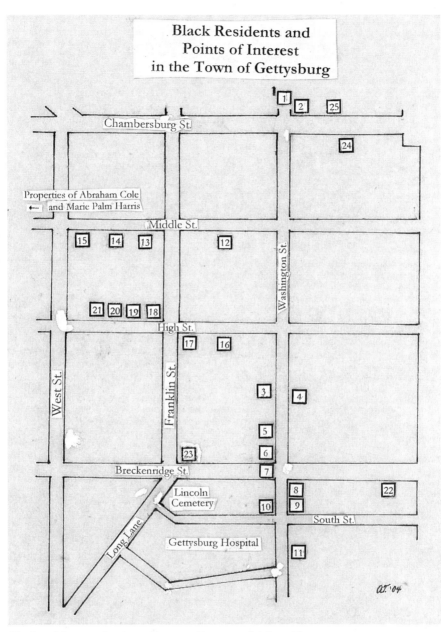

Black Residents and Points of Interest in the Town of Gettysburg

Chambersburg St.

Properties of Abraham Cole and Marie Palm Harris

Middle St.

Washington St.

High St.

West St.

Franklin St.

Breckenridge St.

Lincoln Cemetery

Long Lane

Gettysburg Hospital

South St.

Black residents and points of interest. Courtesy of Arleen Thompson.

6. 269 South Washington Street—Singleton Weldon owned a two-story house on the southern half of what is now church property; Ann Chiller shared the house with him.
7. South Washington and Breckenridge streets—on present-day street surface of Breckenridge, directly south of 269 South Washington, Sidney O'Brien owned a one-story frame house. At the time of the battle, Breckenridge Street ended at this intersection.
8. 320 South Washington Street—William G. Jackson owned a two-story frame house.
9. 344 South Washington Street—Jeremiah and Harriet Herrigan owned a story-and-a-half frame house.
10. 415 South Washington Street—Edan Devan owned a story-and-a-half log house. He also owned property at 402 and 400 South Washington.
11. 428 South Washington Street—Josiah Herrigan owned a story-and-a-half frame house.
12. 124 West Middle Street—Adam Drowry owned a house here.
13. 210 West Middle Street—Matilda Erb was the nonresident owner of this property.
14. South side of third block of West Middle Street, one block east of West Street—Elizabeth Constance owned a one-story frame house.
15. West Middle and West streets, southeast corner—Tracy McGibbon owned a one-story frame house.
16. 124 West High Street—Owen Robinson owned a story-and-a-half frame house and shop. Robinson was the sexton of the Presbyterian church. He successfully maintained a small restaurant, selling oysters in the winter and ice cream of his own making in the summer.
17. West High and Franklin streets, southeast corner (Agricultural Hall)—black abolitionist and editor Frederick Douglass once delivered an address here (see historical marker)
18. West High and Franklin streets, northwest corner—site of "Colored School" (see historical marker).
19. 225–27 West High Street—Sarah Thomas owned a story-and-a-half house.
20. 229 West High Street—Julia Jenkins owned a story-and-a-half frame house.

21. 231 West High Street—William and Amanda McGee owned a story-and-a-half frame house.
22. 28 Breckinridge Street—Nathan and Sarah Bell leased this house and shared it with William and Nancy Crawford.
23. 145 West Breckinridge Street—Harriet Stanton, widow of U.S. Colored Troops veteran Samuel M. Stanton, lived here when she was about eighty years of age. In a letter to the pension board, she explained that she did not know her exact age, because she had been sold on the auction block when she was only a young girl (see Figure 6.1).
24. 30 Chambersburg Street (Christ Lutheran Church)—newspaper and memoir sources indicate that this church may have been used to conceal black citizens of Gettysburg during the first Confederate occupation of the town.
25. Chambersburg Street—site of pre–Civil War law office of Thaddeus Stevens, vigorous white abolitionist and champion for civil rights for blacks. Stevens was chief architect of the Fourteenth Amendment to the U.S. Constitution, guaranteeing citizenship and equal protection of the law regardless of race (see historical marker).

Beyond the Map

Abraham Cole and his family owned a house near West Middle Street, with property extending onto the eastern slope of Seminary Ridge. Marie Palm Harris owned a one-story frame house along West Middle Street; the land adjoined the rear of Abraham Cole's property. Sophia Devan owned a story-and-a-half house at 230 Steinwehr, the southwestern corner of the intersection of Taneytown Road. Emanual and Elizabeth Fox leased half of Sophia Devan's house.

I am indebted to Gerald R. Bennett, who has spent years pouring over tax rolls and other public records trying to compile a comprehensive list of the residents of Gettysburg at the time of the battle and identify their place of residence. He has generously shared the fruits of his labor.

~

Bibliography

Archival Sources

Adams County Historical Society
Biggs Family File.
Elwood W. Christ, "Pennsylvania History Resources Form for 201 South Washing-
    ton Street," 1989.
Gettysburg School Board Minutes.
"Gettysburg Schools," "Teachers in the Colored Schools."
Jacob Melchoir Sheads, "Re-burial of Union Dean in the National Cemetery."
Mary Elizabeth Monfort File, "How a Twelve-Year-Old Girl Saw Gettysburg."
McCauslin, Debra Sandoe, "Black Civil War Veterans from Biglerville."
Palm Family File.

Gettysburg National Military Park Library and Archives
Vertical Files.
William Gladstone Collection.

Historical Society of Pennsylvania
Abraham Barker Collection.
George W. Fahnestock.

National Archives

Record Group 92
Records of Quartermaster Department, Entry 238: Reports of Persons and Articles
Hired (Oversize File), 1863; Capt. John McHarg, Frederick, MD, vol. 2, Report of
Deceased and Discharged with Salary Due (July–December), July 19, 1863.

Record Group 94
Adjutant General's Office Miscellaneous File ("Colored Troops").
Camp William Penn Letters.
Individual Pension Records.
Individual Service Records.
Records of Movements and Activities of Volunteer Organizations.

Record Groups 79T and 79TM
Still Pictures, Battle of Gettysburg and Gettysburg National Military Park.

Record Group 107
Records of the Office of the Secretary of War, Entry 32: Letters Received from the
Commissary General of Prisoners (selected items).

U.S. Army Military History Institute
Harrisburg Civil War Round Table Collection.
Gettysburg Civilian Files.
Robert L. Brake Collection.
Steljes Collection.

Published Primary Sources

Alleman, Tillie (Pierce). *At Gettysburg.* New York: W. Lake Borland, 1889.
Basler, Roy P. *The Collected Works of Abraham Lincoln.* 9 vols. New Brunswick, NJ:
Rutgers University Press, 1953–1955.
Bergeron, Arthur W., Jr. "Free Men of Color Fought for South." *Washington Times,*
January/February 1993.
Berlin, Ira, Joseph P. Reidy, and Leslie S. Rowland, eds. "Freedom: A Documentary
History of Emancipation, 1861–1867." In *The Black Military Experience,* 2nd ser.,
vol. 1. New York: Cambridge University Press, 1982.
Blackett, R. J. M., ed. *Thomas Morris Chester, Black Civil War Correspondent: His Dis-
patches from the Virginia Front.* Baton Rouge: Louisiana State University Press, 1989.
Blackford, W. W. *War Years with Jeb Stuart.* New York: Scribner's, 1946.
Brown, William Wells. *The Negro in the American Rebellion: His Heroism and His
Fidelity.* New York: Lee and Shepard, 1867; reprint, Boston: Lee and Shepard
Johnson, 1968.

Buehler, Fannie J. *Recollections of the Rebel Invasion and One Woman's Experiences during the Battle of Gettysburg*. Privately published, 1896.

Caba, G. Craig, ed. *Episodes of Gettysburg and the Underground Railroad: As Witnessed and Recorded by Professor J. Howard Wert*. Gettysburg, PA: privately published, 1998.

Cormany, Rachel. "Diary, Letters and Diaries, Franklin County, Pennsylvania." In *Valley of the Shadow: Two Communities in the American Civil War*. Charlottesville: University of Virginia, Virginia Center for Digital History.

Cree, Jemima K. "Letter." In *Kittochtinny Papers, 1905–1908*. Chambersburg, PA.

Creigh, Reverend Thomas. "Letters and Diaries, Franklin County, Pennsylvania." In *Valley of the Shadow: Two Communities in the American Civil War*. Charlottesville: University of Virginia, Virginia Center for Digital History.

Dunaway, Wayland Fuller. *Reminiscences of a Rebel*. New York: Neale, 1913.

Emilio, Luis F. *A Brave Black Regiment: History of the Fifty-fourth Regiment of Massachusetts Volunteer Infantry*. Boston: Boston Book, 1894.

Fasnacht, Mary Warren. *Memories of the Battle of Gettysburg, Year 1863*. New York: Princely, 1941.

Freemantle, Arthur J. L. *Three Months in the Southern States*. 1864; reprint, Lincoln: University of Nebraska Press, 1991.

Goss, Warren Lee. *Recollections of a Private: A Story of the Army of the Potomac*, illustrations by J. R. Chapin. New York: Crowell, 1890.

Hanifen, Michael. *History of Battery B, First New Jersey Artillery*. Ottawa, IL: Longstreet House, 1905 (reprinted 1991).

Herbert, T. W., ed. "In Occupied Pennsylvania." *Georgia Review* (summer 1950).

Heyser, William. Diary. "Letters and Diaries, Franklin County, Pennsylvania." In *Valley of the Shadow: Two Communities in the American Civil War*. Charlottesville: University of Virginia, Virginia Center for Digital History.

Heysinger, Isaac W. *Antietam and the Maryland and Virginia Campaigns of 1862*. New York: Neale, 1912.

Higginson, Thomas Wentworth. *Army Life in a Black Regiment*. Fields, Osgood, 1810; reprint, Boston: Beacon, 1962.

Hoke, Jacob. *The Great Invasion of 1863*. Dayton, OH: Shuey, 1887; reprint, New York: Yoseloff, 1959.

———. *Historical Reminiscence of the War: In and about Chambersburg during the War of the Rebellion*. Chambersburg, PA, 1884.

Jacobs, M. "Notes on the Rebel Invasion of Maryland and Pennsylvania and the Battle of Gettysburg." *Pilot*, July 28, 1863.

Johnson, Robert U., and Clarence C. Buel, eds. *Battles and Leaders of the Civil War*. 4 vols. New York: Century, 1884–1888.

McCreary, Albertus. "Gettysburg: A Boy's Experience of the Battle." *McClure* 33 (July 1909): 243–45.

McCurdy, Charles M. *Gettysburg: A Memoir*. Pittsburgh, PA: Reed & Witting, 1929.

McMurray, John. *Recollections of a Colored Troop*. Brookville, PA, 1916.

McPherson, James M. *The Negro's Civil War: How American Negroes Felt and Acted during the War for the Union*. New York: Vintage Books, 1965.

Moore, Frank, ed. *Rebellion Record: A Diary of American Events, with Narratives, Illustrative Incidents, Poetry, Etc.* 8 vols. New York: Putnam, 1861–1866.

Myers, Betty Dorsey. *Segregation in Death: Gettysburg's Lincoln Cemetery*. Gettysburg, PA: Lincoln Cemetery Project Association, 2001.

Norton, Oliver Wilcox. *Army Letters, 1861–1865*. 1903; reprint, Dayton, OH: Morningside, 1990.

Payne, Daniel Alexander. *Recollections of Seventy Years*. Nashville, TN: AME Sunday School Union, 1888; reprint, New York: Arno, 1969.

Redkey, Edwin S., ed. *A Grand Army of Black Men*. Cambridge, MA: Cambridge University Press, 1992.

Rodgers, Sarah Sites. *The Ties of the Past: The Gettysburg Diaries of Salome Myers Stewart, 1854–1922*.

Rozier, John, ed. *The Granite Farm Letters: The Civil War Correspondence of Edgeworth & Sallie Bird*. Athens: University of Georgia, 1988.

Schaff, Philip. "Gettysburg Week." *Scribner's* 16 (July 1894): 22–25.

Sherman, William T. *Memoirs of General William T. Sherman*. Bloomington: Indiana University Press, 1957.

Smedley, Robert Clemens. *History of the Underground Railroad in Chester and Neighboring Countries of Pennsylvania*. Lancaster, PA: Office of the Journal, 1883; reprinted as *History of the Underground Railroad* (New York: Arno, 1969).

Still, William. *A Brief Narrative of the Struggle for the Rights of the Colored People of Philadelphia in the City Railway Cars*. Philadelphia: Merrihew, 1867.

Taylor, Frank H. *Philadelphia in the Civil War, 1861–1865*. Philadelphia: City of Philadelphia, 1913.

Williams, George W. *A History of the Negro Troops in the War of the Rebellion 1861–1865*. New York: Harper & Brothers, 1888; reprint, New York: Negro Universities Press, 1969.

Wilson, Joseph T. *The Black Phalanx*. Hartford, CT: American, 1890; reprint, New York: Arno and New York Times, 1968.

Lectures, Tours, and Interviews

Bearss, Edwin C. "Retreat and Pursuit after Gettysburg." Tour, Gettysburg College Civil War institute, June 24, 2003.

Brown, Kent Masterson. "Retreat and Pursuit." Lecture delivered at Gettysburg College Civil War Institute, June 23, 2003.

Caba, Craig. "Gettysburg and the Underground Railroad." Lecture delivered at United Sates Colored Troops Institute, National Civil War Museum, Harrisburg, Pennsylvania, September 21, 2002.

Kross, Gary. "Cemetery Hill." Tour sponsored by the Lincoln Forum, Gettysburg, 1998, recorded by C-Span Television.

Myers, Betty. "History of Blacks in Adams County." Lecture on audiotape, recorded February 7, 1989, Adams County Historical Society.

Shultz, Dean. "McAllister Mill and the Underground Railroad." Tour, Gettysburg College Civil War Institute, June 26, 2003.

Vermilyea, Peter C. "Gettysburg: The African American Experience." Tour, Gettysburg College Civil War Institute, June 26, 2003.

Weigley, Russell F. "African Americans in the Civil War." Lecture delivered at Civil War Symposium, Cabrini College, Radnor, Pennsylvania, October 2000.

Government Publications

The War of the Rebellion: A Compilation of the Official Records of the Union and Confederate Armies, 4 series, 70 vols. Washington, DC: Government Printing Office, 1880–1891.

Newspapers

Anglo-African.
Christian Recorder.
Daily (Lancaster) *Evening Express.*
Franklin Repository (Franklin County, PA).
(Gettysburg) *Compiler.*
(Gettysburg) *Star and Sentinel.*
Harrisburg Daily Telegraph.
Harrisburg Patriot and Union.
Harrisburg Sunday Telegraph.
(New York) *Herald.*
Philadelphia Inquirer, June 26, 1863–November 19, 1863.
(Philadelphia) *Press*, June 25, 1863–October 5, 1863.
(Philadelphia) *Public Ledger*, June 18, 1863–October 5, 1863.
Pottersville Miners' Journal.
Valley Spirit (Franklin County, PA).

Electronic Sources

Anderson, Osborne P. *A Voice from Harpers Ferry.* Boston. www.libraries.wvu.edu/theses/Attfield/HTML/voice.html.

Emile Davis Diaries, 1863–1865. Pennsylvania State University Libraries. www.libraries.psu.edu/psul/digital/davisdiaries.html.

Petruzzi, J. David. *Buford's Boys: The Internet's Most Complete Resource of Buford's Calvary in the American Civil War.* www.bufordboys.com.

Schaefer, Thomas L. *Defend or Destroy? The Columbia-Wrightsville Bridge in the Gettysburg Campaign.* Video disc and videotape. Rivertownes, PA: Total Magic Video Production.

Valley of the Shadow: Two Communities in the American Civil War. Charlottesville: University of Virginia, Virginia Center for Digital History. http://valley.vcdh.virginia.edu.

Secondary Sources

Alexander, Ted. "A Regular Slave Hunt." *North and South* 4, no. 7 (September 2001).

———. "Ten Days in July: The Pursuit to the Potomac." *North and South* 2, no. 6 (August 1999): 10–34.

Ayers, Edward L. *In the Presence of Mine Enemies*. New York: Norton, 2003.

Basler, Roy P. "Did President Lincoln Give the Smallpox to William H. Johnson?" *Huntington Library Quarterly* 35, no. 3 (May 1972): 279–84.

Bates, Samuel P. *History of Pennsylvania Volunteers, 1861–5*. 5 vols. Harrisburg, PA: Singerly, State Printer, 1869–1871.

Bennett, Gerald R. *Days of "Uncertainty and Dread": The Ordeal Endured by the Citizens of Gettysburg*. Camp Hill, PA, 1994; reprint, Camp Hill, PA: Plank's Suburban, 1997.

Bergeron, Arthur W., Jr. "Louisiana's Free Man of Color." In *Black Southerners in Gray: Essays on Afro-Americans in Confederate Armies*, edited by Richard Rollins. Redondo Beach, CA: Rank and File, 1994.

Biddle, Daniel R., and Murray Dubin. *Tasting Freedom: Octavius Catto and the Battle for Equality in Civil War America*. Philadelphia: Temple University Press, 2010.

Binder, Frederick M. "Pennsylvania Negro Regiments in the Civil War." *Journal of Negro History* 37 (October 1952).

Blair, William, and William Pencak. *Making and Remaking Pennsylvania's Civil War*. University Park: Pennsylvania State University Press, 2001.

Blassingame, John W. "Negro Chaplains in the Civil War." *Negro History Bulletin* 27, no. 21 (October 1962): 23–24.

Blight, David W. *Race and Reunion: The Civil War in American Memory*. Cambridge, MA: Harvard University Press, 2001.

Blockson, Charles L. *African Americans in Pennsylvania: A History and Guide*. Baltimore: Black Classic, 1994.

———. *African Americans in Pennsylvania: Above Ground and Underground, an Illustrated Guide*. Harrisburg, PA: RB Books, 2001.

———. "Escape from Slavery: The Underground Railroad." *National Geographic* 166, no. 1 (July 1984).

———. *The Underground Railroad in Pennsylvania*. Jacksonville, NC: Flame International, 1981.

Bloom, Robert L. *A History of Adams County, Pennsylvania, 1700–1990*. Gettysburg, PA: Adams County Historical Society, 1992.

Boatner, Mark M., III. *The Civil War Dictionary*. New York: McKay, 1959.

Boritt, G. S. *The Gettysburg Gospel: The Lincoln Speech That Nobody Knows*. New York: Simon & Schuster Paperbacks, 2008.

———, ed. *The Gettysburg Nobody Knows*. New York: Oxford University Press, 1997.

Brewer, James H. *The Confederate Negro: Virginia's Craftsmen and Military Laborers, 1861–1865*. Durham, NC: Duke University Press, 1969.

Brodie, Fawn M. *Thaddeus Stevens: Scourge of the South*. New York: Norton, 1959.

Brown, Kent Masterson. *Retreat from Gettysburg: Lee, Logistics, and the Pennsylvania Campaign*. Chapel Hill: University of North Carolina, 2005.

Coco, Gregory A. *Strange and Blighted Land: Gettysburg, the Aftermath of a Battle*. Gettysburg, PA: Thomas, 1995.

———. *A Vast Sea of Misery: A History and Guide to the Union and Confederate Field Hospitals at Gettysburg, July 1–November 23, 1863*. Gettysburg, PA: Thomas, 1988.

———. *Wasted Valor*. Gettysburg, PA: Thomas, 1990.

Coddington, Edwin B. *The Gettysburg Campaign: A Study in Command*. New York: Scribner's, 1968.

Conrad, W. P., and Ted Alexander. *When War Passed This Way*. Greencastle, PA: Greencastle Bicentennial, 1982.

Cornish, Dudley T. *The Sable Arm: Negro Troops in the Union Army*. New York: Longmans Green, 1956; reprint, Lawrence: University Press of Kansas, 1987.

Creighton, Margaret S. *The Colors of Courage: Gettysburg's Hidden History. Immigrants, Women, and African-Americans in the Civil War's Defining Battle*. New York: Basic, 2005.

Dryer, Brainerd. "The Treatment of Colored Troops by the Confederates, 1861–1865." *Journal of Negro History* 20 (July 1935): 273–86.

Dusinberre, William. *Civil War Issues in Philadelphia, 1856–1865*. Philadelphia: University of Pennsylvania Press, 1965.

Faust, Patricia L., ed. *Historical Times Illustrated Encyclopedia of the Civil War*. New York: Harper & Row, 1986.

Fields, Barbara Jeanne. *Slavery and Freedom on the Middle Ground: Maryland during the Nineteenth Century*. New Haven: Yale University Press, 1985.

Foner, Philip S. "The Battle to End Discrimination against Negroes in Philadelphia Streetcars: Part I." *Pennsylvania History* 15, no. 3 (July 1973): 261–90; "The Battle to End Discrimination against Negroes in Philadelphia Streetcars: Part II." *Pennsylvania History* 15, no. 4 (October 1973): 355–79.

Frassanito, William A. *Early Photography at Gettysburg*. Gettysburg, PA: Thomas, 1995.

———. *Gettysburg: A Journey in Time*. New York: Scribner's, 1975.

Freeman, Douglas Southhall. *Lee's Lieutenants*. 3 vols. New York: Scribner's, 1944.

French, Steve. *Imboden's Brigade in the Gettysburg Campaign*. Hedgesville, WV: French, 2008.

Gannon, Barbara A. "Sites of Glory: African-American Grand Army of the Republic Posts in Pennsylvania." In *Making and Remaking Pennsylvania's Civil War*, edited by William Blair and William Pencak. University Park: Pennsylvania State University Press, 2001.

Gladstone, William A. *Men of Color*. Gettysburg, PA: Thomas, 1993.

———. *United States Colored Troops*. Gettysburg, PA: Thomas, 1990.

Glatfelter, Charles H. *The Churches of Adams County, Pennsylvania: A Brief Review and Summary*. Giblerville, PA: St. Paul's Lutheran Church, 1987.

———. *A Salutary Influence: Gettysburg College 1832–1985*. Gettysburg, PA: Gettysburg College, 1987.

Glatthaar, Joseph T. *Forged in Battle: The Civil War Alliance of Black Soldiers and White Officers*. New York: Free Press and Collier Macmillan, 1990.

Guthrie, James M. *Campfires of the Afro-American*. Philadelphia: Afro-American, 1899; reprint, New York: Johnson, 1970.

Gwaltney, William W. "New Market Heights." In *The Civil War Battlefield Guide*, edited by Frances H. Kennedy. Boston: Houghton Mifflin for the Conservation Fund, 1990.

Hargrove, Hondon B. *Black Union Soldiers in the Civil War*. Jefferson, NC: McFarland, 1988.

Johnson, Clifton. *Battleground Adventures*. Boston: Houghton Mifflin, 1916.

Jones, Shelley L., and Harry Stokes. *Black History in Our Community*. Gettysburg, PA.

Jordan, Ervin L., Jr. *Black Confederates and Afro-Yankees in Civil War Virginia*. Charlottesville: Union Press of Virginia, 1995.

Krick, Robert K. *The Fredericksburg Artillery*. Lynchburg, VA: Howard, 1986.

Levine, Bruce. "In Search of a Usable Past: Neo-confederates and Black Confederates." In *Slavery and Public History: The Tough Stuff of American Memory*, edited by James Oliver Horton and Lois E. Horton. New York: New Press, 2006.

Matthews, Harry Bradshaw. *Re-visiting the Battle of Gettysburg, Pa.: The Presence of African Americans before and after the Conflict*. Oneonta, NY, 1995.

———. *Whence They Came: Families of United States Colored Troops in Gettysburg, Pennsylvania, 1815–1871*. 1992.

McCauslin, Debra Sandoe. *Reconstructing the Past: Puzzle of the Lost Community at Yellow Hill*. Gettysburg, PA: For the Cause, 2007.

McFeeley, William S. *Frederick Douglas*. New York: Norton, 1955.

———. *Yankee Stepfather: General O. O. Howard and the Freedmen*. New York: Norton, 1968.

McLaughlin, Jack. *Gettysburg: The Long Encampment*. New York: Bonanza Books, 1963.

Miers, Earl Schenek, and Richard A. Brown, eds. *Gettysburg*. Rev. ed. New York: Collier Books, 1962.

Miller, William J. *The Training of an Army: Camp Curtin and the North Civil War*. Shippensburg, PA: White Mane, 1990.

Mingus, Scott L. *Flames beyond Gettysburg: The Gordon Expedition June 1863. A History and Tour Guide*. Columbus, OH: Ironclad, 2009.

Moebs, Thomas Truxton. *Black Soldiers, Black Sailors, Black Ink: Research Guide on African Americans in U.S. Military History, 1526–1900*. 4 vols. Chesapeake, VA: Moebs, 1994.

Montgomery Horace. "A Union Officer's Recollections of the Negro as a Soldier." *Pennsylvania History* 28 (April 1961).

Moore, Frank, ed. *The Rebellion Record: A Diary of American Events*. 12 vols. 1861–1866; reprint, New York: Arno, 1977.

Moss, Juanita Patience. *The Forgotten Black Soldiers in White Regiments during the Civil War*. Westminster, MD: Heritage, 2004.

Nagle, George F. *The Year of Jubilee: Men of Muscle*. Vol. 2. 2010.

Nelson, Truman. *The Old Man: John Brown at Harpers Ferry*. Toronto: Holt, Reinhart and Winston of Canada, 1973.

Nevins, Alan. *Ordeal of the Union*. 4 vols. New York: Scribner's, 1975.

Nye, Wilbur S. *Here Come the Rebels!* Baton Rouge: Louisiana State University Press, 1965.

Paradis, James M. *Strike the Blow for Freedom: The Sixth United States Colored Infantry in the Civil War*. Shippensburg, PA: White Mane, 1998.

Pfanz, Harry W. *Gettysburg: The First Day*. Chapel Hill: University of North Carolina Press, 2001.

———. *Gettysburg: The Second Day*. Chapel Hill: University of North Carolina Press, 1987.

Powell, Walter L. *The Alexander Dobbin House: A Short History*. Gettysburg, PA, 1989.

Quarles, Benjamin. *The Negro in the Civil War*. New York: Russell and Russell, 1953.

Redkey, Edwin S. "Black Chaplains in the Civil War." *Civil War History* 22, no. 4 (December 1987).

Rinaldi, Harriette C. *Born at the Battlefield of Gettysburg: An African-American Family Saga*. Princeton, NJ: Markus Wiener, 2004.

Rollins, Richard. "Black Confederates at Gettysburg." *Gettysburg Magazine* 6 (January 1992).

———, ed. *Black Southerners in Gray: Essays on Afro-Americans in Confederate Armies*. Redondo Beach, CA: Rank and File, 1994.

Ross, Fitzgerald. *Cities and Camps of the Confederate States*. Champaign: University of Illinois Press, 1958.

Sauers, Richard A. *Advance the Colors: Pennsylvania Civil War Battle Flags*. Harrisburg, PA: Capitol Preservation Committee, 1987.

Schildt, John W. *Roads from Gettysburg*. Shippenburg, PA: Burd Street Press, 1998.

Silcox, Harry C. "Nineteenth Century Philadelphia Black Militant: Octavius V. Catto (1839–1871)." *Pennsylvania History* 44, no. 1 (January 1977).

Slaughter, Thomas P. *Bloody Dawn: The Christiana Riot and Racial Violence in the Antebellum North*. New York: Oxford University Press, 1991.

Slawson, Robert G. *Prologue to Change: African Americans in Medicine in the Civil War Era*. Frederick, MD: NMCWM, 2006.

Smith, Eric Ledell. "The Civil War Letters of Quartermaster Sergeant John C. Brock, 43rd Regiment, United States Colored Troops." In *Making and Remaking Pennsylvania's Civil War*, edited by William Blair and William Pencak. University Park: Pennsylvania State University Press, 2001.

Smith, John David, ed. *Black Soldiers in Blue: African American Troops in the Civil War Era*. Chapel Hill: University of North Carolina Press, 2002.

Sommers, Richard J. "The Dutch Gap Affair: Military Atrocities and Rights of Negro Soldiers." *Civil War History* 21 (1975): 51–64.

Switala, William J. *The Underground Railroad in Pennsylvania*. Mechanicsburg, PA: Stackpole Brooks, 2001.

Trudeau, Noah A. *Like Men of War: Black Troops in the Civil War, 1862–1865*. Boston: Little, Brown, 1998.

Vermilyea, Peter C. "The Effect of the Confederate Invasion of Pennsylvania on Gettysburg's African American Community." *Gettysburg Magazine* 24 (January 2001).

———. "Jack Hopkins' Civil War." *Adams County History* 11 (2005): 4–21.

Washington, John E. *They Knew Lincoln*. New York: Dutton, 1942.

Weigley, Russell F. "The Border City in the Civil War, 1854–1865." In *Philadelphia: A 300-year History*, edited by Russell F. Weigley. New York: Norton for the Barre Foundation, 1982.

———. "Emergency Troops in the Gettysburg Campaign." *Pennsylvania History* 25, no. 1 (January 1958): 39–57.

Wert, Jeffry D. "Camp William Penn and the Black Soldier." *Pennsylvania History* 46, no. 4 (October 1979).

Westwood, Howard C. *Black Troops, White Commanders, and Freeman During the Civil War*. Carbondale: Southern Illinois University Press.

Whiteman, Maxwell. *Gentlemen in Crisis: The First Century of the Union League of Philadelphia, 1862–1962*. Philadelphia: Union League, 1975.

Wills, Garry. *Lincoln at Gettysburg: The Works that Remade America*. New York: Simon & Schuster, 1992.

Dissertations and Theses

Johnson, James Elton. "A History of Camp William Penn and Its Black Troops in the Civil War, 1863–1865." PhD dissertation, University of Pennsylvania, 1999.

Whitted, Burma L. "The History of the Eighth United States Colored Troops." MA thesis, Howard University, 1960.

Index

Abbott, Alexander Ruffin, 77
Adams County Anti-Slavery Society, 5
Adams County Courthouse, 2, 5
Adams Sentinel, 104
African Americans. *See* blacks
African Methodist Episcopal (AME)
Church, 2, 3–4, 34, 103, 104, 117.
See also Bethel AME Church; St.
Paul AME Zion Church
Alabama, O'Neal's Brigade, 63
Alexander, Edward P., 71
AME. *See* African Methodist Episcopal
Church
American Revolution, 22
Anderson, George "Tige," 57
Anderson, Joseph G., 42
Andersonville, 7, 94
Andrew, John, 39, 40
Anglo-African, 36
Antietam, Battle of, 60, 83
Appomattox Court House, Virginia,
100, 109
Arkansas, 57, 76
Arlington National Cemetery, 86
Armstrong, William, 94

Army of Northern Virginia, 95; at
Battle of Wrightsville, 53–54;
Cavalry Division, 20–21, 44;
foraging, 31, 58, 63; seizing blacks
in Pennsylvania, 31–39; surrender
of, 100
Army of the James, 95
Army of the Potomac, 61, 95; I Corps,
117; II Corps, 59; III Corps (*see*
Birney, David B.; Sickles, Daniel E.);
IX Corps, 95; XI Corps, 55; Cavalry,
60, 64–65, 72
Artillery Reserve, 61–62, 119
Asbury Church, 2
Ashe, Charlotte, 84
Augusta, Alexander T., 77, 78. *See also*
photospread
"Aunt Beckie," 34
Avery, Isaac E., 72

Baltimore, Maryland, 82, 86
Baltimore Pike, 6, 7, 61
Baltimore Street, 5, 34
Bares, Amos, 38
Barksdale, William, 90

Pennsylvania: 3rd Pa. Cavalry, 75;
   27th Pa. Emergency Volunteers,
   51–54; 83rd Pa., 58; black troops
   from, 39–43, 44–45, 48–49, 51–55,
   93–101; gradual emancipation, 1–2;
   seizing blacks in, 9, 31–39; slavery
   in, 1–2
Pennsylvania College, 3, 9, 10, 11,
   35, 82, 106, 115, 117, 123. See also
   Hopkins, "Jack"
Pensacola, Florida, 22, 95
Petersburg, Virginia, 95–97, 100
Pettigrew, James J., 72–73
Philadelphia, Pennsylvania, 34, 75, 90;
   black troops from, 40–43
Philadelphia Inquirer, 44
Philkill, John, 32
Pickett, George E., 39
Pickett's Charge, 1, 59–60, 62, 72, 118,
   120
Pierce, Tillie, 34
Point Lookout, Maryland, 94
Port Hudson, Louisiana, 23
Portsmouth, Virginia, 77, 103
Porter, P. A., 87
Potomac River, 61. See also Falling
   Waters; Williamsport
Pottsville Miners' Journal, 53
Powell, James I., 19
Presbyterian Church, 2, 38
prisoners of war: blacks guarding
   Confederates, 94; Confederate policy
   toward black POWs, 19; Union
   policy toward black POWs, 86–89
prisons: Andersonville, 7, 94; for
   civilians seized in the North,
   38; Fort McHenry, 86–89; Point
   Lookout, 94
Purvis, Charles Barleen, 77

Quaker Valley, Pennsylvania, 8,
quartermaster: Confederate, 63, 72;
   Union, 15–16, 61, 63

railroads, 49; B & O Station, D.C., 101;
   black employees, 37; Cumberland
   Valley RR, 37; Pennsylvania
   Central RR, 54; Pennsylvania
   RR, 43; Petersburg, 95; repairing
   destroyed track, 75; unfinished,
   10, 11; Western Maryland Station
   (Gettysburg), 82
Rapier, John, 77
Reading Daily Times, 53
Redding, John T., 93, 100
Redding, Mary, 100
Reed, Samuel A., 94
Republican Party, 84
reunions, GAR, 108–9. See also
   photospread
Reynolds, John F., 117, 90, 118
Rhode Island, 111–12
Richmond, Virginia, 24, 38, 77, 95
Rideout, Harrison, 94
Rigby, James H., 61
Robertson, James M., 62
Robinson, David A., 93
Robinson, Owen, 4, 106, 120, 125
Rock Creek, 4, 6, 61
Rockville, Maryland, 20
Rodes, Robert E., 63
Rogers, J. B., 19
Rogers, Levi, 94
Rose, John, house, 57
Royer, Nelson, 75, 94, 100
Russell, Aaron, 120

Sandoe, George Washington, 7
Savannah, Georgia, 78
Schaff, Rev. Dr. Philip, 31–32, 38
Schmucker, Dr. Samuel S., 3
Schneck, Rev. Dr. Benjamin, 37
schools: in Charleston, South Carolina,
   3; in Gettysburg, 3, 4, 8, 104, 107,
   125; Granite School, 59
Scott, Alexander, 94, 100
Scott, Dred, 86

~

About the Author

James M. Paradis completed his bachelor degree at LaSalle University in Philadelphia in 1971 and his master and doctoral degrees in history at Temple University. His doctoral dissertation became the basis for his first book, *Strike the Blow for Freedom: The 6th United States Colored Infantry in the Civil War*, published in 1998 and released in paperback in 2000. He currently teaches history at Arcadia University and at Doane Academy in Burlington, New Jersey, where he has taught for over twenty years and serves as dean of the Upper School. His second book, *African Americans and the Gettysburg Campaign*, was published in 2005. At the invitation of the National Parks Service, he addressed the annual meeting of licensed battlefield guides, Gettysburg, Pennsylvania, on the role of African Americans in the Gettysburg Campaign. Dr. Paradis has served for many years on the board of directors of Citizens for the Restoration of Historical La Mott, which is charged with the preservation of the site of Camp William Penn and the reopening of its museum of U.S. Colored Troops. He served as historical consultant and narrator for the documentary film *Black Soldiers in Blue: The Story of Camp William Penn* (2009). This work led to a commendation from the Cheltenham Branch of the NAACP.